THE GOSPEL ACCORDING TO THOMAS

*Seek this wisdom by doing service, by strong search, by
questions, and by humility; the wise who see the truth will
communicate it unto thee, and knowing which thou shalt
never fall into error.*

SHRI KRISHNA

SACRED TEXTS

GENERAL EDITOR

RAGHAVAN IYER

This series of fresh renderings of sacred texts from the world's chief religions
is an inspiring testament to the universality of the human spirit. Each text is
accompanied by an instructive essay as an aid to reflection. In the ancient
world, before the proliferation of print, seekers of wisdom thought it a great
privilege to learn a text, and sought oral instruction from a Teacher in the
quest for enlightenment. The scriptures of all traditions are guides to the
attainment of serene continuity of consciousness through the practice of
self-study, self-transcendence and self-regeneration in daily life.

SACRED TEXTS

RETURN TO SHIVA (from the *Yoga Vasishtha Maharamayana*)

THE GATHAS OF ZARATHUSTRA — The Sermons of Zoroaster

TAO TE CHING by Lao Tzu

SELF-PURIFICATION (Jaina Sutra)

THE DIAMOND SUTRA (from the Final Teachings of the Buddha)

THE GOLDEN VERSES OF PYTHAGORAS
(with the commentary of Hierocles)

IN THE BEGINNING — The Mystical Meaning of Genesis

THE GOSPEL ACCORDING TO THOMAS
(with complementary texts)

THE SEALS OF WISDOM — The Essence of Islamic Mysticism
by Ibn al-'Arabi

CHANTS FOR CONTEMPLATION by Guru Nanak

THE GOSPEL ACCORDING TO THOMAS

The *Gospel According to Thomas* was discovered in 1947 amongst the Nag Hammadi manuscripts in Egypt. Whilst the entire library of long lost codices sheds new light on the origins of the Christian tradition, this brief gospel might well be the earliest record of the utterances of Jesus. Accessible to the agnostic as well as the mystic, these one hundred and fourteen stanzas are compellingly rendered by Pico Iyer in the spirit of the original Coptic. The aphoristic text is illuminated by additional selections from Gnostic Christian sources. Two instructive essays, "The Mystery of Christos" by H.P. Blavatsky and "The Message of Jesus" by Raghavan Iyer, are accompanied by two introductory articles, "The Gnostic Transmission" and "Gnostic Theogony" by Elton Hall. The poem "The Voice Divine" by Louis Claude de Saint Martin concludes the selections. A glossary of terms is included.

THE GOSPEL
ACCORDING
TO
THOMAS

WITH COMPLEMENTARY TEXTS

CONCORD GROVE PRESS
1983

CONCORD GROVE PRESS
London   Santa Barbara   New York

First Edition: December 25, 1983

ISBN 0-88695-005-8

10 9 8 7 6 5 4 3

Printed in the United States of America

CONTENTS

PART I

THE GNOSTIC TRANSMISSION   6

THE GOSPEL ACCORDING TO THOMAS   17

THE MYSTERY OF CHRISTOS   44

THE MESSAGE OF JESUS   52

PART II

GNOSTIC THEOGONY   69

TREATISE ON THE RESURRECTION   74

APOCRYPHON OF JOHN   78

EVANGELIUM VERITATIS   97

SONG OF THE PEARL   119

THE VOICE DIVINE   126

GLOSSARY   129

Even though myself unborn, of changeless essence, and the lord of all existence, yet in presiding over nature — which is mine — I am born but through my own maya, *the mystic power of self-ideation, the eternal thought in the eternal mind. I produce myself among creatures, O son of Bharata, whenever there is a decline of virtue and an insurrection of vice and injustice in the world; and thus I incarnate from age to age for the preservation of the just, the destruction of the wicked, and the establishment of righteousness. Whoever, O Arjuna, knoweth my divine birth and actions to be even so doth not upon quitting his mortal frame enter into another, for he entereth into me. Many who were free from craving, fear, and anger, filled with my spirit, and who depended upon me, having been purified by the ascetic fire of knowledge, have entered into my being. In whatever way men approach me, in that way do I assist them; but whatever the path taken by mankind, that path is mine, O son of Pritha.*

SHRI KRISHNA

Once unfettered, delivered from their dead-weight of dogmatism, interpretations, personal names, anthropomorphic conceptions, and salaried priests, the fundamental doctrines of all religions will be proved identical in their esoteric meaning. Osiris, Krishna, Buddha, Christ, will be shown as different means for one and the same royal highway of final bliss — Nirvana. Mystical Christianity teaches *self*-redemption through one's own seventh principle, the liberated Paramatma, called by the one Christ, by others Buddha; this is equivalent to regeneration, or rebirth in spirit, and it therefore expounds just the same truth as the Nirvana of Buddhism. All of us have to get rid of our own Ego, the illusory, apparent self, to recognise our true Self, in a transcendental divine life. But if we would not be selfish we must strive to make other people see that truth, and recognise the reality of the transcendental Self, the Buddha, the Christ, or God of every preacher.

THE MAHA CHOHAN

THE GNOSTIC TRANSMISSION

The days of Constantine were the last turning-point in history, the period of the Supreme struggle that ended in the Western world throttling the old religions in favour of the new one, built on their bodies. From thence the vista into the far distant Past, beyond the 'Deluge' and the Garden of Eden, began to be forcibly and relentlessly closed by every fair and unfair means against the indiscreet gaze of posterity. Every issue was blocked up, every record that hands could be laid upon, destroyed. Yet there remains enough, even among such mutilated records, to warrant us in saying that there is in them every possible evidence of the actual existence of a Parent Doctrine. Fragments have survived geological and political cataclysms to tell the story; and every survival shows evidence that the now Secret Wisdom was once the one fountain head, the ever-flowing perennial source, at which were fed all its streamlets – the later religions of all nations – from the first down to the last. This period, beginning with Buddha and Pythagoras at the one end and the Neo-Platonists and Gnostics at the other, is the only focus left in History wherein converge for the last time the bright rays of light streaming from the aeons of time gone by, unobscured by the hand of bigotry and fanaticism.

The Secret Doctrine, I, xliv-xlv

The excitement surrounding the discovery of the Dead Sea Scrolls overshadowed two other momentous discoveries which, unlike the Scrolls, penetrate to the core of Christianity. Ancient manuscripts exhumed in the Near East often pass through many clandestine hands — always for a price — before entering the public arena. Their origins may never be known, and their place of burial may be obliterated forever. Occasionally, however, careful sleuthing provides clues. The Dead Sea Scrolls were apparently discovered in 1947 by a shepherd boy in a cave high above the Dead Sea near ancient Qumran. They were sealed in earthen jars by the inhabitants of that isolated community in about 68 A.D. when the Tenth Roman Legion entered the area to suppress the First Jewish Revolt. The ascetic brotherhood of Qumran was probably Essene and philosophically related to the *Therapeutai.*

In the same year the first part of a large Coptic Gnostic library was discovered in Egypt. Eventually thirteen codices were recovered, containing forty-nine manuscripts. While some of them were previously known, at least in part, they presented a panorama of Gnostic teaching which brilliantly illumines the early evolution of Christianity. Apparently they were found in an earthen jar in a grave near Nag Hammadi about sixty miles from Luxor. In the mountain Gebel el-Tarif are seven tombs of Sixth Dynasty pharaonic princes. Here the ascetic Palamun taught Pachomius, who in turn founded the order of Coptic monasticism which spread throughout Egypt. Here also the Greek city of Diospolis Parva flourished as capital of Upper Egypt, across the Nile from Shenesit ('the acacias of Seth'), which became Chenoboskion and later Nag Hammadi. The stern ascetic Fathers vigorously purged every pagan vestige from this area, but Gnostic 'heresies' sprang up with equal strength. The grave in which the Gnostic library was found had been dug in the fourth century, after the abandonment of Nag Hammadi by Christian monasticism. One of the documents in this collection is the *Gospel According to Thomas.*

Eleven years after these discoveries, in 1958, Morton Smith was looking through the library of the oldest Christian monastery still in use, Mar Saba, situated in a Dead Sea *wadi* about fifteen miles from Qumran. In the back of Isaac Voss' 1646 edition of the letters of St. Ignatius of Antioch, he found a letter of Clement of Alexandria. It is the only known extant letter of Clement, and it refers to and quotes from the *Secret Gospel of Mark.*

Gnostic schools — only a few of which used the appellation — held that the redemption of humanity is possible only through *gnosis* or knowledge of reality. *Gnosis* in its philosophical meaning is 'enlightenment,' the full intuitive awakening of consciousness to its spiritual origin and source. Jesus and others had the *gnosis* and freely imparted it to those who were ready, but many who heard did not understand because their minds were beclouded by *agnosia* or ignorance. While the details of Gnostic cosmogony vary with the school, there is an underlying unity of thought. The Ever-Hidden Deity — *deus absconditus* — radiates *pleroma*, the divine, perfect and archetypal fullness. Within *pleroma* a hierarchical sequence of primordial polarities emerge. These intelligent potencies, *syzygies*, give rise to the manifest universe. Potential spirit and matter manifest as *pneuma* and *hyle*. In some systems, aeons and archons preside over the successively emerging planes of being, each more differentiated than its parent. The aeons are the intelligent centres of spiritual force which link planes of being with *pleroma*, while the archons preside over their material evolution. Being ignorant of their own glorious origin, they look away from the divine. Gnostics familiar with Judaeo-Christian scriptures taught that the stern and jealous God Jehovah is the lowest archon, presiding over the psycho-physical world. The Father in the teachings of Jesus, they held, is not this archon, but the divine source of the *pleroma* itself, the unmanifest Cause. Man, as a self-conscious being, must choose between them, since *psyche*, self-consciousness, links them together. If *psyche* identifies with the perishable physical man, it becomes more deeply enmeshed in matter, a divine luminous spark locked in a prison of darkness. But if *psyche* identifies with its pneumatic Self, man gains *gnosis* and is redeemed through self-consciously entering the divine *pleroma*. Redemption is the total transformation of man from an ephemeral being into an immortal spiritual entity, a living temple of the *Christos*. In the words of Paul, all men of *gnosis*

> . . . have put on the *new man* which is renewed in knowledge after the image of him who created him: where there is neither Greek nor Jew, circumcision nor uncircumcision, Barbarian, Scythian, bond nor free: but Christos is all, and in all.
>
> *Colossians*, 3:10-11

The universal Gnostic vision, united in aim and spirit with the authentic Mysteries of every age and culture, was eventually lost by the church. *Gnosis* — difficult to achieve but infinitely valuable — was displaced by *sacrament* — easy to obtain from priests for a price. The early Church Fathers treated the Gnostics as heretics, accusing them of a demonic inversion of orthodoxy and perversion of Christian rites. The Gnostics, however, arose in ancient times and only later became associated with Christian heresies. Scholars have been unwilling to trace their ultimate origins on the ground that the empirical evidence is conflicting and fragmentary. Some say the Gnostics were derived from the Iranian fire mysteries. Zoroastrians influenced the Jews during the

Babylonian captivity to the extent that Cyrus the Great, a
Zoroastrian, is called the shepherd of God in the *Old Testament.*
The Gnostic language of light and darkness, the teaching of the
Unnameable Father, and the cosmic significance of human conduct
have affinities with oriental religious philosophy. The Hellenic
concern with the Hermetic channels between the divine and
human realms, the deific personifications and the inner temple
mysteries are equally reflected in Gnostic doctrine. The early
Kabbalah — especially the Sephirothal Tree — and the Essene
affirmation of the Teachers of Righteousness are closely related
to the Gnostic hierarchy of wisdom as told in the wanderings of
Sophia. Gnosticism embraced a broad association of groups, each
gathered around a Teacher who had attained some insight into
gnosis. They recognized one another by the spirit of their doctrines
and life rather than through the comparison of catechisms. *Gnosis*
as a state entails preparation, purgation and purification including
self-restraint in mind and body and the cultivation of the spiritual
will. As knowledge, it is transmitted within the sanctified secrecy
of the relationship of Teacher and disciple. When the disciple has
become like a clear, smooth receptive mirror, the Wisdom-light
which radiates through the Teacher shines upon him and fills him
with light. Earned on the one hand and granted on the other, the
gnosis of disciple and Teacher is subsumed in the irreversible law
of spiritual transmission. With the emergence of Christianity,
Gnostics within and without the church naturally adopted the
clothing of Christian language, tailored to their own conceptions,
which they held were those of the great Gnostic Teacher Jesus.
Seven centuries later, the pre-Islamic *sufis* would similarly adopt
the language and outer form of Islam.

The Gnostic mysteries were an embarrassment to the church,
for it wished to win over the uncultured masses on the one hand
and become a political force on the other. Its bid for popularity
and power left little room for a doctrine of truth through
renunciation, universal love and mutual toleration. The desire to be
influential in the world prevented its bishops from taking up the
quiet and arduous path of inner transformation. By the time of
Clement of Alexandria (d. 203 A.D.), the tension between those
who knew or at least sensed the mysteries, and those who were
building a new empire, had become severe. Clement was torn

10

between loyalty to the small core of Initiates and an attraction to making converts in vast numbers. He could not bring himself to risk losing either. Hence, he could neither stem the tide against Christian *gnosis* nor wholeheartedly give himself to dogma. His vacillation cost him both Gnostic support and posthumous Christian sainthood.

The church's claim to be the unique possessor and guardian of wisdom was utterly unacceptable to Gnostics within and outside its fold. This insult to the beneficence of Nature and blasphemy against the sacred names of Masters of Wisdom in every race and time were vigorously challenged by the Gnostic movement. The church declared Gnostics heretics and embarked on a program to revise history to suit its purposes. It took the costumes of the Vestal Virgins and the title of their head — *Pontifex Maximus* — along with the Egyptian Madonna and Child — Isis and Horus — and the Mithraic communion, only to disfigure them all and proffer them as original sacramental mysteries. By the end of the third century, Gnostic movements had mostly dispersed, though their teachings persisted through history like a thorn in the papal paw — Manichaeism in Byzantium, Paulicians in Rome, the Albigenses in France. While its vivifying and ameliorating effect was shunned and lost by the church, the torch of *gnosis* was never allowed to burn out.

At the turn of the century, researchers sifting the soil of the once great city of Oxyrhynchus in Upper Egypt uncovered numerous fragments of papyrus. Three of the Oxyrhynchus papyri contain *logia* (sayings) of Jesus not found in the canonical gospels. Some scholars suspected that these fragments belonged to one collection passed down outside the canon. The discovery of the *Gospel According to Thomas* revealed the source of these *logia.*

A fascinating portrait of Thomas emerges from these and other extra-canonical documents. Tradition calls him Didymus Judas Thomas, the twin brother of Jesus as well as his most intimate disciple. After Jesus departed from the world and the disciples spread out in every direction to bring the gospel — the 'good news' — to humanity, Thomas went to India. Today, the St. Thomas Christians, an Indian church, trace their origins back to Thomas.

'Doubting' Thomas is often thought of as the weakest of the disciples because he questioned whether the being who appeared to the disciples after the resurrection was Jesus.

> But Thomas, one of the twelve, called Didymus, was not
> with them when Jesus came. The other disciples therefore
> said unto him, We have seen the Lord. But he said unto
> them, Except I shall see in his hands the print of the nails,
> and put my finger into the print of the nails, and thrust
> my hand into his side, I will not believe.
>
> *John*, 20:24-25

Eight days later he had the opportunity to do so. The Gnostic
documents do not portray a vacillating Thomas. Rather, he is
initiated into the Mysteries by Jesus as a spiritual companion.
Presumably his 'doubt' is the insistence on seeing firsthand the
marks of the Initiate, symbolically given as the wounds suffered
in the crucifixion.

The *Gospel According to Thomas* begins: "These are the secret
words spoken by the Living Jesus and recorded by Didymus Judas
Thomas." The word 'Living' in Gnostic literature refers to Jesus
after the resurrection, that is, after the three days in the tomb.
The story of the crucifixion, entombment and resurrection of Jesus
is the story of sacred initiation. Jesus the *Chréstos* became Jesus
the *Christos*. H.P.Blavatsky wrote, "*Chréstos* was the lonely traveller
journeying on to reach the ultimate goal through that 'Path,'
which goal was *Christos*, the glorified Spirit of 'TRUTH,' the reunion
with which makes the soul (the Son) ONE with the (Father)
Spirit." In language to which every ancient Gnostic would assent,
she adds:

> Christos is the crown of glory of the suffering Chréstos of
> the mysteries, as of the candidate to the final UNION, of
> whatever race and creed. To the true follower of the
> SPIRIT OF TRUTH, it matters little, therefore, whether Jesus,
> as man and Chréstos, lived during the era called Christian,
> or before, or never lived at all. The Adepts, who lived and
> died for humanity, have existed in many and all the ages,
> and many were the good and holy men in antiquity who
> bore the surname or title of Chréstos before Jesus of
> Nazareth, otherwise Jesus (or Jehoshua) Ben Pandira was
> born. Therefore, one may be permitted to conclude, with
> good reason, that Jesus, or Jehoshua, was like Socrates, like
> Phocian, like Theodorus, and so many others surnamed
> *Chréstos, i.e.,* the 'good, the excellent,' the gentle, and the
> holy Initiate, who showed the 'way' to the Christos

condition, and thus became himself 'the Way' in the hearts of his enthusiastic admirers.

The *Gospel According to Thomas* is one of several writings found at Nag Hammadi in which Jesus and his disciples appear. Like the *Wisdom of Jesus*, the *Apocryphon of John* and the *Gospel of Philip*, it constitutes a bridge between the canonical gospels, proffered as the basis of orthodoxy, and those Gnostic works which do not consider Jesus and his disciples. In the *Gospel According to Thomas*, two themes are threaded through one central event. There is frequent reference in the *logia* to Light, suggesting an ontology common to all Gnostics, and numerous analogies are drawn to illustrate the meaning of the Kingdom of Heaven, a concept found in the canon and in Essene documents. In the midst of his explication of these two themes, Jesus initiates Thomas.

Light is the manifest veil which covers the Hidden Deity in every religious tradition. Light is the first period ('day') of creation in *Genesis*. The Egyptian Atum is the first bubble of light in Infinite Darkness. It divides itself into two halves — Shu and Tefnut, Life and Order — just as the Hindu Brahma arises as Hiranyagarbha, the effulgent Golden Egg, to emit Vach and Viraj, the creative and archetypal sides of Nature. "In the beginning was the Word," John wrote, "and the Word was with God, and the Word was God." The Logos (Word) emerges from Darkness and is Light. "And the light shineth in darkness, and the darkness comprehended it not," for the Hidden Deity stands out of all relation to manifestation. Atum is life, light, substance and consciousness, according to the Egyptians, while John said, "In him was life, and the life was the light of men." The highest Logoic radiance is in every human being though it is unperceived. Hence Jesus says in the *Gospel According to Thomas* (*logion* 50), "If you are asked your origins, answer: 'We have come out of the Light where the Light came of itself.' "

When Jesus asked his disciples to compare him with someone, Simon Peter likened him to an angel and Matthew to a philosopher. But Thomas said that he could not make any comparison. Jesus responded, "You have drunk from the bubbling fountain which I brought" (*logion* 13) and took Thomas aside from the other disciples. He gave Thomas three words of great potency — *mantrams*. In this initiation lies the key to the unique position of Thomas in

Gnostic literature: Jesus transmitted the *gnosis* to Thomas who had demonstrated himself worthy of it.

Clement's letter to Theodore on the *Secret Gospel of Mark* is suggestive in this regard. Theodore had heard rumours of a secret gospel and made inquiries. In response, Clement explained that Mark had come to Alexandria and while there had added to his gospel "the things suitable to whatever makes for progress toward *gnosis*." When Mark was dying, "he left his composition to the church in Alexandria, where it even yet is most carefully guarded, being read only to those who are being initiated into the great mysteries." After noting some of the erroneous impressions garnered by Theodore, Clement quotes a passage from the *Secret Gospel* reminiscent of John's story of the raising of Lazarus.

> And they came into Bethany, and a certain woman, whose brother had died, was there. She came and prostrated herself before Jesus and said to him, 'Son of David, have mercy on me.' But the disciples rebuked her. And Jesus, being angered, went off with her into the garden where the tomb was, and at once a great cry was heard from the tomb. Going near, Jesus rolled away the stone from the door of the tomb. Immediately going in where the youth was, he stretched forth his hand and raised him, seizing his hand. The youth, looking upon Jesus, loved him, and began to beseech him that he might be with him. Leaving the tomb, they entered the house of the youth — who was rich. And after six days Jesus told him what to do: in the evening the youth came to him, wearing only a linen cloth over his nudity. He remained with Jesus that night, for Jesus taught him the mystery of the Kingdom of God.

According to Clement of Alexandria, the mystery of Initiation, preserved in the Gnostic sanctuaries until their destruction by bigoted orthodoxy, can be traced directly to Jesus. The esoteric Christianity of the Gnostics was the vital core of the teachings of Jesus.

For the Gnostic, as for Clement of Alexandria, who "was an Initiate, a new Platonist, before he became a Christian," the Kingdom of Heaven is not an eschatological promise fulfilled for the blind believer ritualistically redeemed only after death: rather it is a present reality which can be witnessed by the purified and prepared consciousness. The Kingdom of Heaven is the self-conscious abiding in the realization of the Light in which we live and move and have our being. It ever was, is, and will be. Jesus says, "The Sanctuary you expect is here, although you cannot recognize it" (*logion* 51), and "the Kingdom of the Father is spread throughout the earth and no man sees it" (*logion* 113). The *Gospel According to Thomas* invites us to seek it within, to enter into it, and to offer it to all humanity.

Words can merely clothe the ideas, but no number of words can convey an idea to one who is incapable of perceiving it. Every one of us has within him the latent capacity or a sense dormant in us which can take cognisance of Abstract Truth, although the development of that sense or, more correctly speaking, the assimilation of our intellect with that higher sense, may vary in different persons, according to circumstances, education and discipline. That higher sense which is the potential capacity of every human being is in eternal contact with Reality, and every one of us has experienced moments when, being for the time *en rapport* with that higher sense, we realise the eternal verities. The sole question is how to focalise ourselves entirely in that higher sense.

DAMODAR K. MAVALANKAR

THE GOSPEL ACCORDING TO THOMAS

These are the secret words
Spoken by the Living Jesus,
And recorded by Didymus Judas Thomas.

1. Jesus said:
    He who uncovers
    The significance of these words
    Shall not taste death.

2. Let him who seeks,
    Not cease from his search
    Until he finds.
    When he finds, he will be bewildered,
    And, when bewildered,
    He will wonder, and reign over the All.

3. If your guides claim
    That the Kingdom is in the sky,
    The birds of the sky will be there before you.
    If they say that it is in the sea,
    The fishes of the sea will be there before you.
    The Kingdom is within you and without you.
    When you know yourselves, you will be known.
    Then, you shall know that you are
    Sons of the Living Father.
    But, if you do not know yourselves
    You are in poverty, and you are poverty.

4.   An old man, heavy in years,
Will not hesitate
To ask a baby, seven days old,
About the Place of Life.
And he shall live, for many
Who are first shall be last,
United within the Single One.

5.   Jesus said:
      Know what is before you.
That which is hidden will be revealed.

6.   His Disciples asked Him:
"Do you want us to fast?
How should we pray
And distribute alms?
What rules should we observe in eating?"
Jesus replied:
      Do not lie.
Do not do what you dislike,
For all is revealed before Heaven.
Everything hidden will be revealed.
Nothing covered will remain undiscovered.

7.   Blessed is the lion
Eaten by a man, so that
It becomes a man.
Profane is the man
Eaten by a lion,
So that he becomes a lion.

8.   Man is like a skilful fisherman,
Casting his net into the sea
And drawing it out replete with small fish.

If the wise fisherman finds amongst them a large fish
He throws the smaller back into the sea,
Having selected the largest with ease.
He who has ears to hear, let him hear.

9. Jesus said:
A sower came forth,
Filled his hands, and cast.
A few seeds fell upon the road, where
Birds came down and devoured them.
Others fell among thorns,
Where they choked, or were eaten by worms.
Still others fell upon good ground,
Where they could bring forth good fruit.

10. Jesus said:
I have cast
A fire upon the world,
And I rekindle it
Until it burns.

11. This Heaven shall pass away
And that above shall pass away.
The dead no longer live.
The living no longer die.
When you ate good things
It was you who gave them life.
But what are you going to do in the Light?
When you were One
You were made Two, but when you are Two,
What are you going to do?

12. The Disciples said to Jesus:
"We know that you are to leave us.

Which of us is to be leader?"
Jesus replied:
   Whenever you have gone
You will go to James the Just
For whom
Heaven and Earth came into being.

13.   Jesus addressed his Disciples:
   Compare me to someone.
Tell me whom I resemble.
Simon Peter said:
"Like a just Angel."
Matthew answered:
"Like a wise philosopher."
But Thomas replied:
"Truly, Master, my mouth
Cannot bring itself to utter comparisons."
And Jesus said:
   I am no longer your Master.
You have drunk from the bubbling fountain
Which I brought,
And you are drunk —
He took Thomas aside,
And said three words to him.
When Thomas returned,
His companions asked:
"What did Jesus tell you?"
And he replied:
"If I related even one of the words
He told me,
You would gather stones,
And hurl them at me, whereupon fire would leap from
The stones, and burn you."

14.   Jesus said:

      If you fast,
You will create sins for yourselves.
If you pray, you will be condemned.
If you give alms, you will injure yourselves.
If you go into a land and wander
Throughout its area,
And are offered hospitality,
Eat what is set before you.
Heal the sick amongst them.
It is not
What goes into your mouth that defiles you
But what comes out of your mouth that defiles you.

15.   When you perceive
One not born of woman,
Prostrate yourselves
And worship Him. He is your Father.

16.   Men think that
I came to bring peace to the world.
They do not know that
I bring division,
Fire and sword and war.
There shall be five in a house
With three against two
And two against three;
The father against the son,
And the son against the father,
And they shall stand alone.

17.   Jesus said:

      I shall give you
What no eye has seen,

No ear heard, no hand touched
Nor any heart received.

18.   The Disciples said to him:
"Warn us how our end will be."
Jesus replied:
    Have you already discovered
The Beginning, now that
You are asking about the end?
Wherever the Beginning is,
There shall be the end.
Blessed is he who stands
At the Beginning, for he understands
The end without tasting death.

19.   Blessed is he
Who was, before he became.
If you become my Disciples
And respond to my words,
Stones will rise to your service.
You have five trees in Paradise,
Immobile during summer and winter,
Never shedding their leaves.
He who knows them all
Shall never taste death.

20.   The Disciples challenged Him:
"Tell us what the Kingdom of Heaven is like."
He answered:
    The Kingdom of Heaven is like
A grain of mustard.
Although smaller than all other seeds,
When it falls upon tilled earth,

It sends forth a great branch,
Which becomes a splendid harbour for birds.

21. Mary Magdalen asked Jesus:
"What are your Disciples like?"
He said:
     They are like children
Settled in a field not theirs.
When the owners of the field
Approach them, and order,
'Give us back our field!'
They will be naked before them, and
Will hand it over.
So, I say to you:
If a householder is aware
That a thief is coming,
He will await his arrival,
Block his way into the house,
The Kingdom, and so protect his property.
Be wary of the world.
Gird your loins in strength
So that no robbers enter,
For the benefits you expect
Will be found: may there rise among you
A man of understanding.
When the fruit is ripening,
He comes with his swift sickle,
And reaps.
He who has ears to hear, let him hear.

22. Jesus saw little ones being fed.
He addressed his Disciples:
     These babies being nursed
Are like those entering the Kingdom.

They asked: "Shall we enter the Kingdom?
We are small."
Jesus said:
　When you make two into one
And what is within like what is without,
And what is without like what is within.
And what is above like what is below,
And when you unite male and female in one
So that the male is no longer male,
And the female no longer female,
When you make eyes in place of an eye
And a hand in place of a hand,
And a foot in place of a foot
And an image in place of an image,
Then you shall enter the Kingdom.

23.　　I shall choose
One from a thousand,
And two from ten thousand,
And they shall stand in unity.

24.　　His Disciples requested:
"Teach us about the Place
Where you live,
For we must seek it."
He said:
　He who has ears to hear, let him hear.
There is Light in a Man of Light,
Who gives Light to the World.
If he does not give Light,
There is only Darkness.

25.　　Love your brother
Like your own soul. Cherish him
Like the apple of your eye.

26.   You see the mote
Within your brother's eye,
But you do not see the beam
Within your own.
Once you have extracted the beam
From your own eye,
You can remove the mote
From your brother's.

27.   Unless
You abstain from the world,
You will not find the Kingdom.
Unless you honour the Sabbath,
You will not see the Father.

28.   I stood
In the midst of the world.
I appeared incarnate
And I found everyone drunk,
And none thirsty.
Then my Soul was sorry
For all the sons of men,
Because they are blind in their hearts.
They cannot realize that they have come
Empty into the world,
And must leave it empty.
Now, they are drunk,
But when they renounce the wine,
They will repent.

29.   If the Flesh
Came into Being for the sake
Of the Spirit, that is
A Mystery. But if

26

The Spirit came into Being
For the sake of the Body,
That is a wondrous Miracle.
How did such great wealth
Make its home, I wonder,
In such poverty?

30.   Where there are three Gods,
They are Gods.
Where there are two, or one,
I am with Him.

31.   No prophet is honoured
In his homeland.
No physician heals those
Who know him well.

32.   No city
Built high upon a mountain,
And well fortified,
Can fall, or conceal itself.

33.   Jesus said:
Whatever you hear,
With one ear and the other,
Preach from the housetops.
Nobody lights a lamp in order
To place it under a bushel
Or to hide it in some secret place.
Set it upon a lampstand,
So that all who enter or depart
May see its light.

34.   When the blind lead the blind,
They fall together into the ditch.

35.   Nobody can enter
The house of a strong man,
Or seize it by force,
Unless his hands are tied.
Only then can the house
Be ransacked.

36.   Morn to Eve, and Eve to Morn
Do not think what you shall put on.

37.   His Disciples asked: "When will you appear to us
And when shall we see you?"
Jesus answered:
    When you shed your shame, and take your clothes,
Place them on the ground, and trample them underfoot
Like children. Then you will see
The Son of the Living One, and will not be afraid.

38.   You have often wished
To hear the words
I now express.
When you have no other to listen to,
Days will come when you shall search,
But never find me.

39.   The Scribes and Pharisees
Received the keys of understanding, and hid them.
They did not enter, nor allowed entrance to
Those who so wished.
Be wise as serpents, and innocent as doves.

40.   A vine was planted outside the Father,
Yet, as it was never tethered,
It was torn by the roots, and died.

28

41.   He who has something in his hands,
Will receive, and from him
Who has nothing, shall be taken away
All that he possesses.

42.   Jesus said:
    Be passers-by.

43.   His Disciples said:
"Who are you to say that to us?"
He replied:
    You do not understand
Who I am, from what I say.
You have become like the Jews.
They love the Tree and hate the Fruit.
You love the Fruit and hate the Tree.

44.   He who blasphemes against the Father
Shall be forgiven, and he who blasphemes against the Son
Shall be forgiven, but he who blasphemes against the
Holy Ghost
Shall not be forgiven on Earth or in Heaven.

45.   No grapes
Are gathered from thorn,
Nor are figs plucked from camelthorn.
A good man produces good from his treasure.
An evil man brings forth evil from his heart,
Speaking evil when he expresses himself.

46.   Jesus said:
    From Adam
To John the Baptist,
None born of woman is higher

Than John the Baptist, whose
Eyes remain unbroken.
Whoever becomes small
Shall understand the Kingdom,
And be exalted above John.

47.   A man cannot mount two horses,
Or bend two bows.
A servant cannot obey two masters, for
He must honour the one, and despise the other.
Nobody at once drinks old wine, and desires new.
Nor is new wine packed within old skins,
Lest they crack.
Old wine is not contained within new skins,
Lest they perish.
An old patch is not grafted upon new clothes,
For it will tear.

48.   If two
Make peace with one another in the same house,
They can order the mountain to move,
And it will move.

49.   Jesus said:
Blessed are the solitary, and the Elect
For they shall discover the Kingdom from which
They come, and to which they must return.

50.   If you are asked your origins, answer:
'We have come out of the Light
Where the Light came of itself.
It rested, appearing in their Image.'
If you are asked your identity, answer:
'We are His sons, and

The Elect of the Living Father.'
If asked for a sign of your Father, answer:
'Movement and Repose.'

51.   His Disciples asked Jesus:
"When will begin the Repose of the Dead?
And when will the new world appear?"
He answered:
    The Sanctuary you expect is here,
Although you cannot recognize it.

52.   His Disciples commented:
"Twenty-four prophets spoke in Israel.
All referred to you."
Jesus replied:
    You have
Neglected the one who lives
In your presence, in order to
Talk about the dead.

53.   His Disciples asked:
"Is circumcision of use?"
He said:
    If it were useful,
Your father would have begotten you
Circumcised out of your mother.
But the real circumcision of the Spirit
Has always been useful,
And nothing but useful.

54.   Blessed are the poor,
For theirs is the Kingdom of Heaven.

55.   Jesus said:
    He who does not hate

Father and Mother cannot be my Disciple,
As he who does not hate brother and sister,
And take up his cross as I did,
Cannot ever become worthy of me.

56.   He who has known the world
Has found a corpse,
And the world is unworthy of him
Who has found a corpse.

57.   The Kingdom of the Father
Is like a farmer who possessed good seed.
One night, his enemy sowed
Tares among the seed, but the farmer
Refused to pull up the tares, saying:
'You might uproot wheat as well.'
On the harvest day, the tares
Will appear, be uprooted, and burned.

58.   Blessed is the man who has suffered,
For he has truly discovered life.

59.   Look to the Living One
As long as you live, lest you die,
Then search for him, and fail.

60.   A Samaritan was bearing a lamb towards Judea.
Jesus asked his Disciples why he wanted the animal.
They replied that he wished to kill and to eat it.
He replied:
    As long as it is alive,
He will not eat it.
He can eat only once it is dead.
"There is no other way," they said.

He answered:

    You too are seeking rest in order to
Avoid becoming corpses, and ripe for being eaten.

61.   Two share one bed.
One shall live, and the other die.
Salome challenged him, "Who are you?
Did you mount my bed,
And eat from my table?"
Jesus addressed her:
    I am an equal.
I have been given things
Belonging to my Father.
Salome replied, "I am your Disciple."
And Jesus responded:
    When a man is growing equal,
He shall be suffused with Light,
But when he is growing apart,
He shall be consumed with Darkness.

62.   Jesus said:
    I reveal my secrets
To those deserving of them.
Do not let your left hand know
What your right is doing.

63.   A rich man owned a great fortune,
And determined to employ it so as to
Sow, reap, plant, and fill his barns
With fruit, that he might lack nothing.
That very night, he died.
He who has ears to hear, let him hear.

64.   Having prepared a banquet,
A host sent his servant to summon the guests.

He went to the first and said:
'My Master has invited you.'
'Some merchants who are in my debt
Are visiting me tonight. I have to advise them.
I am sorry. I cannot come.'
He visited another, and said:
'My Master has sent an invitation to you.'
This one replied:
'I have bought a house, and made
An appointment for today. I have no time.'
He went to another, and offered:
'My Master has invited you.'
He was told:
'My friend is getting married,
And I am organizing a dinner to celebrate.
I cannot come. I must be excused.'
Then he approached another, and said:
'My Master invited you.' He was answered:
'I have just bought an estate, and am about to
Collect the rents. I shall not be able to come.'
The servant returned to his Master, and reported:
'All those you invited are unable to come.'
The Master responded:
'Go into the streets; bring in all you find
To partake of the banquet.
Merchants and dealers shall not enter
The abode of my Father.'

65.   A virtuous man owned a vineyard which he
Gave to farmers to be tilled, having agreed
To receive the fruits from them.
He sent his servant to collect the fruits,
And he was seized, beaten and almost killed.
The servant returned, and told his Master of this.

'Perhaps they did not recognize him,' thought the Master.
So, he sent another servant. The farmers beat him too.
Then, the man sent his Son, thinking
'They will respect my Son.'
The farmers knew that he was heir,
And they seized and killed him.
He who has ears to hear, let him hear.

66.   Show me the stone,
Which the builders rejected.
It is the Head of the Corner.

67.   He who knows the All
And does not know himself
Has missed everything.

68.   You are Blessed,
When men beat you, and persecute you,
For they shall find no place still standing
Where they have tormented you.

69.   Blessed are they who have been persecuted
In their hearts.
They have known the Father in Truth.
Blessed are the hungry,
For he who desires will be satisfied.

70.   When you produce this within,
What you have will save you.
What you do not have within
Will kill you.

71.   Jesus said:
I shall destroy this house,

And nobody will be able to
Restore it.

72.   A man requested:
"Tell my brothers
To divide my Father's things with me."
He replied:
    Who made me a divider?
Turning to his Disciples, he said:
    Do I divide things up?

73.   The harvest is great,
But the labourers are few.
Ask the Lord to send
Labourers to the harvest.

74.   Lord, there are many people
Around the well,
But there is Nobody within the well.

75.   There are many at the door.
But only the solitary ones
Shall enter the Bridal Chamber.

76.   The Kingdom of the Father
Is like a merchant,
Who found a pearl to add to his possessions.
Being a clever merchant,
He sold his other possessions,
And bought himself the pearl alone.
Seek, like him, the treasure
Which does not fade,
In the place where no moths
Enter to consume,
And no worms to corrupt.

77.   Jesus said:
         I am the Light
      That is above them all.
      I am the All.
      The All came from me,
      And the All has returned to me.
      Split wood and I am there.
      Raise a stone and you will find me.

78.   Why have you come into the field?
      To see a reed tremble in the wind?
      To observe a man wearing soft cloth?
      Your kings and great men
      All wear soft clothes, and yet
      They cannot see the truth.

79.   A woman from the crowd addressed him:
      "Blessed is the womb that gave you birth
      And the woman who nursed you."
      He answered:
         Blessed are those who have heard the Word
      Of the Father and maintained it in Truth,
      For the day will come when you will say
      Blessed is the womb which has not conceived,
      And the woman who has not nursed.

80.   He who has known the world,
      Has found the body,
      But he who has found the body,
      Is too great for the world.

81.   He who is rich
      Can become a King.
      He who has power
      Can do without.

82.   He who is close to me
        Is close to fire:
        He who is far from me
        Is distant from the Kingdom.

83.   Images
        Appeared to man, and the Light
        Within is hidden in the Image
        Of the Father's Light.
        He will reveal Himself,
        And his Image hidden by Light.

84.   When you see your likeness,
        You are happy,
        But when you see your images
        Rising before you without subsiding or approaching,
        How long can you stand that?

85.   Adam emerged
        From great power and great wealth,
        And was still unworthy of you.
        Had he been worthy,
        He would not have experienced death.

86.   Foxes have their lairs,
        And birds their nests.
        But the Son of Man has no place
        To lay down his head, and rest.

87.   Wretched is the body
        Dependent upon the body.
        And wretched is the soul
        Dependent upon them both.

88.   Jesus said:
          The Angels and the Prophets
       Shall visit you, and give you
       What is yours.
       For your part, give them
       What you have in your hand
       And ask yourselves when they will come
       To take what is theirs.

89.   Why do you wash
       The surface of the Chalice?
       Do you not understand
       That the man who made the outside
       Also created the inside?

90.   Come to me, for
       My yoke is light,
       My rule is mild
       And you shall find repose.

91.   They said to him:
       "Tell us who you are
       So that we may believe in you."
       He replied:
          You are testing
       The face of Heaven and Earth
       And have not recognized
       The man before you.
       You do not even know
       How to test this moment.

92.   Jesus said:
          Seek and you shall find.
       What you asked me recently,

I did not tell you then.
I want to tell you now,
When you are not asking me.

93.   Do not give the sacred to dogs,
Lest it be cast on the dung-heap.
Do not cast pearls before swine,
Lest they destroy them.

94.   He who seeks shall find
And the doors will be opened to him
Who knocks.

95.   If you have money,
Do not lend it out at interest
But give it to him
Who will not repay it.

96.   The Kingdom of Heaven
Is like a woman who takes a little leaven,
Puts it into dough, and makes large loaves.
He who has ears to hear, let him hear.

97.   The Kingdom of Heaven
Is like a woman carrying a jug
Full of meal on a long journey.
When the handle broke,
The meal streamed out behind her, so that
She never noticed that anything was wrong, until
Arriving home, she set the jug down
And found that it was empty.

98.   The Kingdom of Heaven
Is like a man who wished to assassinate a noble.

He drew his sword at home, and struck it against the wall,
To test whether his hand were strong enough.
Then he went out, and killed the noble.

99.   The Disciples said to Him:
"Your brothers and your mother are outside."
He answered:
    Those who perform
The will of my Father are my brothers and mother.
They are the ones who will enter
My Father's Kingdom.

100.   They showed Jesus a gold coin, and said:
"Caesar's men want tribute from us."
He replied:
    Render unto Caesar
What belongs to Caesar,
And render unto God,
What belongs to God,
And give me what is mine.

101.   He who does not hate
His father and his mother as I do,
Cannot be my Disciple, and he who does not love
His father and mother as I do,
Cannot be my Disciple,
For my Mother killed me,
But my true Mother has given me life.

102.   Woe to the Pharisees.
They resemble a dog in a manger,
Who neither eats, nor allows the oxen to eat.

103.   Blessed is he who knows
The time of the robbers' arrival,

For he can rise, collect himself,
And gird his loins in preparation.

104.   They said:
"Come. Let us pray today, and fast."
Jesus said:
    What sin have I committed?
What have I failed to do?
When the Bridegroom departs
From the Bridal Chamber,
Then you can fast and pray.

105.   He who knows
His Father and his Mother
Shall be called a Bastard.

106.   When you make the two one,
You will become Sons of Man,
And if you order the mountain to move,
It will move.

107.   The Kingdom is like a Shepherd,
Who owned a hundred sheep, the largest of which
Went astray.
He left the ninety-nine, in search of the one
Until he found it. After all his trouble,
He said to the sheep:
'I love you more than the ninety-nine.'

108.   Whoever drinks from my mouth
Shall become as I am.
I too shall become like him.
For him, the hidden will be revealed.

109.   The Kingdom is like a man
Who is ignorant of the treasure
Hidden in his field. When he dies,
He leaves it to his son, who sells it,
Being unaware also of the treasure within.
The buyer will come,
Discover the treasure while ploughing,
And lend out money at interest.

110.   He who has found the world, and riches,
Should then deny the world.

111.   The Heavens shall be rolled back,
And the Earth unfurled before your eyes.
The Living One out of the Living One
Sees neither death, nor fear, for Jesus says
The world is unworthy of the man who finds himself.

112.   Jesus said:
Woe to the flesh
That is dependent upon the Soul,
And woe to the Soul that is
Dependent upon the Flesh.

113.   His Disciples questioned:
"When will the Kingdom come?"
Jesus answered:
It will never come
If you are expecting it.
Nobody will say
Look here or look there.
Yet the Kingdom of the Father
Is spread throughout the earth
And no man sees it.

114.   Simon Peter suggested to them:
"Mary Magdalen should leave us.
Women are unworthy of the Life."
Jesus said:
   I shall lead her
So as to make her a man,
That she may become a
Living Spirit, as you other men,
For every woman made manly,
Shall enter the Kingdom of Heaven.

THE GOSPEL ACCORDING TO THOMAS

THE MYSTERY OF CHRISTOS

TRUTH has not allowed herself to remain without witnesses. There are, besides great Initiates into scriptural symbology, a number of quiet students of the mysteries or archaic esotericism, of scholars proficient in Hebrew and other dead tongues, who have devoted their lives to unriddle the speeches of the Sphinx of the world-religions. And these students, though none of them has yet mastered all the 'seven keys' that open the great problem, have discovered enough to be able to say: There *was* a universal mystery-language, in which all the World Scriptures were written, from *Vedas* to "Revelation," from the "Book of the Dead" to the *Acts*. One of the keys, at any rate — the numerical and geometrical key* to the Mystery Speech is now rescued; an ancient language, truly, which up to this time remained hidden, but the evidences of which abundantly exist, as may be proven by undeniable mathematical demonstrations. If, indeed, the Bible is forced on the acceptance of the world in its dead-letter meaning, in the face of the modern discoveries by Orientalists and the efforts of independent students and kabalists, it is easy to prophesy that even the present new generations of Europe and America will repudiate it, as all the materialists and logicians have done. For, the more one studies ancient religious texts, the more one finds that the ground-work of the New Testament is the same as the ground-work of the Vedas, of the Egyptian theogony, and the Mazdean allegories. The atonements by blood — blood-covenants and blood-transferences from gods to men, and by men, as sacrifices to the gods — are the first keynote struck in every cosmogony and theogony; soul, life and blood were synonymous words in every language, pre-eminently with the Jews; and that blood-giving was life-giving. "Many a legend among (geographically)

---

*"The key to the recovery of the language, so far as the writer's efforts have been concerned, was found in the use, strange to say, of the discovered integral ratio in numbers of diameter to circumference of a circle," by a geometrician. "This ratio is 6,561 for diameter and 20,612 for circumference." (Cabalistic MSS.)

alien nations ascribes soul and consciousness in newly-created mankind to the blood of the god-creators." Berosus records a Chaldean legend ascribing the creation of a new race of mankind to the admixture of dust with the blood that flowed from the severed head of the god Belus. "On this account it is that men are rational and partake of divine knowledge," explains Berosus.* And Lenormant has shown (*Beginnings of History*, p. 52, note) that "the Orphics . . . . said that the *immaterial part of man, his soul* (his life) sprang from the blood of Dionysius Zagreus, whom . . . . Titans tore to pieces." Blood "revivifies the dead" — *i.e.*, interpreted metaphysically, it gives *conscious* life and a soul to the man of matter or clay — such as the modern materialist is now. The mystic meaning of the injunction, "Verily I say unto you, except *ye eat the flesh* of the Son of man and *drink his blood*, ye have not life in yourselves," &c., can never be understood or appreciated at its true *occult* value, except by those who hold some of the *seven keys*, and yet care little for St. Peter.† These words, whether said by Jesus of Nazareth, or Jeshua Ben-Panthera, are the words of an INITIATE. They have to be interpreted with the help of *three* keys — one opening the *psychic* door, the second that of physiology, and the third that which unlocks the mystery of terrestrial being, by unveiling the inseparable blending of theogony with anthropology. It is for revealing a few of these truths, with the *sole view of saving intellectual mankind from the*

*Cory's *Anc. Frag.*, p. 59, f. So do Sanchoniathon and Hesiod, who both ascribe the *vivifying* of mankind to the spilt blood of the gods. But blood and *soul* are one (*nephesh*), and the blood of the gods means here the informing soul.

†The existence of these *seven* keys is virtually admitted, owing to deep research in Egyptological lore, by Mr. G. Massey again. While opposing the teachings of "Esoteric Buddhism" — unfortunately misunderstood by him in almost every respect — in his Lecture on "The Seven Souls of Man," he writes (p. 21) —

"This system of thought, this mode of representation, this septenary of powers, in various aspects, had been established in Egypt, at least seven thousand years ago, as we learn from certain allusions to Atum (the god 'in whom the fatherhood was individualised as the *begetter of an eternal soul*,' the *seventh* principle of the Theosophists), found in the inscriptions lately discovered at Sakkarah. I say in various aspects, *because the gnosis of the Mysteries was, at least, sevenfold in its nature* — it was Elemental, Biological, Elementary (human), Stellar, Lunar, Solar and Spiritual — and *nothing short of a grasp of the whole system can possibly enable us to discriminate the various parts, distinguish one from the other, and determinate the which and the what, as we try to follow the symbolical Seven through their several phases of character.*"

insanities of materialism and pessimism, that mystics have often been denounced as the servants of Antichrist, even by those Christians who are most worthy, sincerely pious and respectable men.

The first key that one has to use to unravel the dark secrets involved in the mystic name of Christ, is the key which unlocked the door to the ancient mysteries of the primitive Aryans, Sabeans and Egyptians. The Gnosis supplanted by the Christian scheme was universal. It was the echo of the primordial wisdom-religion which had once been the heirloom of the whole of mankind; and, therefore, one may truly say that, in its purely metaphysical aspect, the Spirit of Christ (the divine *logos*) was present in humanity from the beginning of it. The author of the Clementine Homilies is right; the mystery of Christos — now supposed to have been taught by Jesus of Nazareth — "was identical" with that which *from the first* had been communicated "*to those who were worthy*," as quoted in another lecture.* We may learn from the Gospel *according to Luke*, that the "worthy" were those who had been initiated into the mysteries of the Gnosis, and who were "accounted worthy" to attain that "resurrection from the dead" *in this life* . . . . "those who knew that they could die no more, being equal to the angels as sons of God and sons of the Resurrection." In other words, they were the great adepts *of whatever religion*; and the words apply to all those who, without being Initiates, strive and succeed, through personal efforts to *live the life* and to attain the naturally ensuing spiritual illumination in blending their personality — (the 'Son') with (the 'Father'), their individual divine Spirit, *the God within* them. This 'resurrection' can never be monopolized by the Christians, but is the spiritual birth-right of every human being endowed with soul and spirit, whatever his religion may be. Such an individual is a *Christ-man*. On the other hand, those who choose to ignore the Christ (principle) within themselves, must die *unregenerate heathens* — baptism, sacraments, lip-prayers, and belief in dogmas notwithstanding.

In order to follow this explanation, the reader must bear in mind the real archaic meaning of the paronomasia involved in the two terms *Chréstos* and *Christos*. The former means certainly more

---

*"Gnostic and Historic Christianity."

than merely 'a good,' and 'excellent man,' while the latter was never applied to any one living man, but to every Initiate at the moment of *his second birth and resurrection.** He who finds Christos within himself and recognises the latter as his only 'way,' becomes a follower and an *Apostle of Christ*, though he may have never been baptised, nor even have met a 'Christian,' still less call himself one.

The word Chréstos existed ages before Christianity was heard of. It is found used, from the fifth century B.C., by Herodotus, by Aeschylus and other classical Greek writers, the meaning of it being applied to both things and persons.

Thus in Aeschylus (Cho. 901) we read of Μαντεύματα πυθόχρηστα (*pythochrésta*) the "oracles delivered by a Pythian God" (*Greek-Eng. Lex.*) through a pythoness; and *Pythochréstos* is the nominative singular of an adjective derived from *chrao* χράω (Eurip. *Ion*, 1,218). The later meanings coined freely from this primitive application, are numerous and varied. Pagan classics expressed more than one idea by the verb χράομαι 'consulting an oracle'; for it also means 'fated,' *doomed* by an oracle, in the sense of a *sacrificial victim to its decree*, or — 'to the WORD'; as *chrésterion* is not only 'the seat of an oracle' but also 'an offering to, or for, the oracle.'† *Chrestés* χρήστης is one who expounds or explains oracles, 'a *prophet*, a *soothsayer*';‡ and *chrésterios* χρηστήριος is one who belongs to, or is in the service of, an oracle, a god, or a 'Master';§ this Canon Farrar's efforts notwithstanding.‖

*"Verily, verily, I say unto thee, except a man *be born again* he cannot see the Kingdom of God." (John iii, 4.) Here the birth *from above*, the spiritual birth, is meant, achieved at the supreme and last initiation.

†The word χρεών is explained by Herodotus (7.11.7) as that which an oracle declares and τὸ χρεών is given by Plutarch (Nic. 14.) as 'fate,' 'necessity.' *Vide* Herod. 7.215; 5.108; and Sophocles, Phil. 437.

‡See Liddell and Scott's Greek-Engl. Lex.

§Hence of a *Guru*, 'a teacher,' and *chela*, a 'disciple,' in their mutual relations.

‖ In his recent work — "The Early Days of Christianity," Canon Farrar remarks: "Some have supposed a pleasant play of words founded on it, as . . . . between *Chrestos* ('sweet' Ps. xxx., iv., 8) and Christos (Christ)" (I. p. 158, *foot-note*). But there is nothing to suppose, since it began by a "play of words," indeed. The name *Christus* was *not* "distorted into Chrestus," as the learned author would make his readers believe (p. 19), but it was the adjective and noun *Chrestos* which became distorted into *Christus*, and applied to Jesus. In a foot-note on the word 'Christian,' occurring in the First

All this is evidence that the terms Christ and Christians, spelt originally *Chrést* and *Chréstians* χρηστιανοι* were directly borrowed from the Temple terminology of the Pagans, and meant the same thing. The God of the Jews was now substituted for the Oracle and the other gods; the generic designation 'Chréstos' became a noun applied to one special personage; and new terms such as *Chréstianoï* and *Chréstodoulos* 'a follower or servant of Chrestos' — were coined out of the old material. This is shown by Philo Judaeus, a monotheist, assuredly, using already the same term for monotheistic purposes. For he speaks of θεόχρηστος (*théochréstos*) 'God-declared,' or one who is declared by god, and of λόγια θεόχρηστα *(logia théochrésta)* 'sayings delivered by God' — which proves that he wrote at a time (between the first century B.C., and the first A.D.) when neither Christians nor Chrestians were yet known under these names, but still called themselves the Nazarenes. The notable difference between the two words χράω — 'consulting or obtaining response from a god or oracle' (χρέω being the Ionic earlier form of it), and χρίω (chrio) 'to rub, to anoint' (from which the name Christos), have not prevented the ecclesiastical adoption and coinage from Philo's expression θεόχρηστος of that other term θεόχριστος 'anointed by God.' Thus the quiet substitution of the letter ι for η for dogmatic

Epistle of Peter (Chap. iv., 16), in which in the *revised* later MSS. the word was changed into *Christian*, Canon Farrar remarks again, "Perhaps we should read the ignorant heathen distortion, *Chrestian*." Most decidedly we should; for the eloquent writer should remember his Master's command to render unto Caesar that which is Caesar's. His dislike notwithstanding, Mr. Farrar is obliged to admit that the name *Christian* was first INVENTED, by sneering, mocking Antiochians, as early as A.D. 44, but had not come into general use before the persecution by Nero. "Tacitus," he says "uses the word Christians with something of apology. It is well known that in the N.T. it only occurs three times, and always involves a hostile sense (*Acts* xi. 26, xxvi. 28 as it does in iv. 16)." It was not Claudius alone who looked with alarm and suspicion on the Christians, so nicknamed in derision for their carnalizing a subjective principle or attribute, but all the pagan nations. For Tacitus, speaking of those whom the masses called 'Christians,' describes them as a set of men *detested for their enormities* and crimes. No wonder, for history repeats itself. There are, no doubt, thousands of noble, sincere, and virtuous *Christian-born* men and women now. But we have only to look at the viciousness of Christian 'heathen' converts; at the *morality* of those proselytes in India, whom the missionaries themselves decline to take into their service, to draw a parallel between the converts of 1,800 years ago, and the modern heathens 'touched *by grace*.'

*Justin Martyr, Tertullian, Lactantius, Clemens Alexandrinus, and others spelt it in this way.

purposes was achieved in the easiest way, as we now see.

The secular meaning of *Chréstos* runs throughout the classical Greek literature *pari passu* with that given to it in the mysteries. Demosthenes' saying ὦ χρηστέ (330, 27), means by it simply "you nice fellow"; Plato (in Phaed. 264 B) has χρηστὸς εἶ ὅτι ἡγεῖ − "you are an excellent fellow to think . . ." But in the esoteric phraseology of the temples 'chrestos,'* a word which, like the participle *chréstheis* is formed under the same rule, and conveys the same sense − from the verb χράομαι ('to consult a god') − answers to what we would call an adept, also a high *chela*, a disciple. It is in this sense that it is used by Euripides (Ion. 1320) and by Aeschylus (IC). This qualification was applied to those whom the god, oracle, or any superior had proclaimed this, that, or anything else. An instance may be given in this case.

The words χρῆσεν οἰκιστῆοα used by Pindar (p. 4-10) mean "the oracle *proclaimed* him the coloniser." In this case the genius of the Greek language permits that the man so proclaimed should be called χρηστός (*Chréstos*). Hence this term was applied to every Disciple recognised by a Master, as also to every good man. Now, the Greek language affords strange etymologies. Christian theology has chosen and decreed that the name Christos should be taken as derived from χρίω χρίσω (Chriso), 'anointed with scented unguents or oil.' But this word has several significances. It is used by Homer, certainly, as applied to the rubbing with oil of the body after bathing (*Il.* 23, 186; also in *Od.* 4, 252) as other ancient writers do. Yet the word χρίστης (*Christes*) means rather a *whitewasher*, while the word Chrestes (χρήστης) means priest and prophet, a term far more applicable to Jesus, than that of the 'Anointed,' since, as Nork shows on the authority of the Gospels, he never

Vide Liddell and Scott's Greek and English Lexicon. *Chrestos* is really one who is continually warned, advised, guided, whether by oracle or prophet. Mr. G. Massey is not correct in saying that ". . . . The Gnostic form of the name Chrest, or Chrestos, denotes the *Good God*, not a human original," for it denoted the latter, *i.e.*, a good, holy man: but he is quite right when he adds that "*Chrestianus* signifies . . . 'Sweetness and Light.' " "The *Chrestoi*, as the *Good People*, were pre-extant. Numerous Greek inscriptions show that the departed, the hero, the saintly one − that is, the 'Good' − was styled *Chrestos*, or the Christ; and from this meaning of the 'Good' does Justin, the primal apologist, derive the Christian name. This identifies it with the Gnostic source, and with the 'Good God' who revealed himself according to Marcion − that is, the Un-Nefer or Good-opener of the Egyptian theology." − (*Agnostic Annual*.)

was anointed, either as king or priest. In short, there is a deep mystery underlying all this scheme, which, as I maintain, only a thorough knowledge of the *Pagan* mysteries is capable of unveiling.* It is not what the early Fathers, who had an object to achieve, may affirm or deny, that is the important point, but rather what is now the evidence for the real significance given to the two terms *Chrêstos* and *Christos* by the ancients in the pre-Christian ages. For the latter had no object to achieve, therefore nothing to conceal or disfigure, and their evidence is naturally the more reliable of the two. This evidence can be obtained by first studying the meaning given to these words by the classics, and then their correct significance searched for in mystic symbology.

Now *Chrêstos,* as already said, is a term applied in various senses. It qualifies both Deity and Man. It is used in the former sense in the Gospels, and in Luke (vi., 35), where it means 'kind,' and 'merciful.' χρηστός ἐστιν ἐπὶ τοὺς, in I Peter (ii., 3) where it is said, "Kind is the Lord," χρηστὸς ὁ κύριος. On the other hand, it is explained by Clemens Alexandrinus as simply meaning a good man; *i.e.,* "All who believe in *Chrêst* (a good man) both *are*, and *are called Chrêstians*, that is good men." (Strom. lib. ii.) The reticence of Clemens, whose Christianity, as King truly remarks in his *Gnostics,* was no more than a graft upon the congenial stock of his original Platonism, is quite natural. He was an Initiate, a new Platonist, before he became a Christian, which fact, however much he may have fallen off from his earlier views, could not exonerate him from his pledge of secrecy. And as a Theosophist and a *Gnostic*, one who *knew,* Clemens must have known that *Christos* was 'the WAY,' while *Chrêstos* was the lonely traveller journeying on to reach the ultimate goal through that 'Path,' which goal was *Christos,* the glorified Spirit of 'TRUTH,' the reunion with which

---

*Again I must bring forward what Mr. G. Massey says (whom I quote repeatedly because he has studied this subject so thoroughly and so conscientiously).

"My contention, or rather explanation," he says, "is that the author of the Christian name is the Mummy-Christ of Egypt, called the *Karest*, which was a type of the immortal spirit in man, the Christ within (as Paul has it), the divine offspring incarnated, the Logos, the Word of Truth, the *Makheru* of Egypt. It did not originate as a mere type! The preserved mummy was the *dead body of any one* that was *Karest*, or mummified, to be kept by the living; and, through constant repetition, this became a type of the resurrection from (not of!) the dead."

makes the soul (the Son) ONE with the (Father) Spirit. That Paul knew it, is certain, for his own expressions prove it. For what do the words πάλιν ὠδίνω ἄχρις οὗ μορφωθῆ χριστὸς ἐνὑμῖν, or as given in the authorised translations, "I am again in travail until *Christ be formed in you*" mean, but what we give in its esoteric rendering, *i.e.*, "until you find *the* Christos within yourselves as your only 'way.' "

Lucifer   H. P. BLAVATSKY
London, 1887

Christ sets His followers no tasks. He appoints no hours. He allots no sphere. He Himself simply went about and did good. He did not stop life to do some special thing which should be called religious. His life was His religion. Each day as it came brought round in the ordinary course its natural ministry. Each village along the highway had someone waiting to be helped. His pulpit was the hillside, His congregation a woman at a well. The poor, wherever He met them, were His clients; the sick, as often as He found them, His opportunity. His work was everywhere; His workshop was the world.

HENRY DRUMMOND

THE MESSAGE OF JESUS

Let us beware of creating a darkness at noonday for ourselves by gazing, so to say, direct at the sun . . . , as though we could hope to attain adequate vision and perception of Wisdom with mortal eyes. It will be the safer course to turn our gaze on an image of the object of our quest.

— The Athenian Stranger
PLATO

Every year more than three hundred and fifty Catholic and Protestant sects observe Easter Sunday, celebrating the Resurrection of Jesus, the Son of God who called himself the Son of Man. So too do the Russian and Greek Orthodox churches, but on a separate calendar. Such is the schism between East and West within Christendom regarding this day, which always falls on the ancient Sabbath, once consecrated to the Invisible Sun, the sole source of all life, light and energy. If we wish to understand the permanent possibility of spiritual resurrection taught by the Man of Sorrows, we must come to see both the man and his teaching from the pristine perspective of Brahma Vach, the timeless oral utterance behind and beyond all religions, philosophies and sciences throughout the long history of mankind.

The *Gospel According to John* is the only canonical gospel with a metaphysical instead of an historical preamble. We are referred to that which was in the beginning. In the New English Bible, the recent revision of the authorized version produced for the court of King James, we are told: Before all things were made was the Word. In the immemorial, majestic and poetic English of the King James version, *In the beginning was the Word and the Word was with God, and the Word was God.* This is a *bija sutra*, a seminal maxim, marking the inception of the first of twenty-one chapters of the gospel, and conveying the sum and substance of the message of Jesus. John, according to Josephus, was at one time an Essene and his account accords closely with the Qumran Manual of Discipline. The gospel attributed to John derives from the same oral tradition as the Synoptics, but it shows strong connections with the Pauline epistles as well as with the Jewish apocalyptic tradition. It is much more a mystical treatise than a biographical narrative.

Theosophically, there is no point or possibility for any man to anthropomorphize the Godhead, even though this may be very touching in terms of filial devotion to one's own physical father. The Godhead is *unthinkable and unspeakable*, extending boundlessly beyond the range and reach of thought. There is no supreme father figure in the universe. In the beginning was the Word, the Verbum, the *Shabdabrahman*, the eternal radiance that is like a veil upon the attributeless Absolute. If all things derive, as St. John explains, from that One Source, then all beings and all the sons of men are forever included. Metaphysically, every human being has more than one father, but on the physical plane each has only one. Over a thousand years or thirty generations, everyone has more ancestors than there are souls presently incarnated on earth. Each one participates in the ancestry of all mankind. While always true, this is more evident in a nation with mixed ancestries. Therefore it is appropriate here that we think of him who preached before Jesus, the Buddha, who taught that we ask not of a man's descent but of his conduct. *By their fruits they shall be known*, say the gospels.

There is another meaning of the 'Father' which is relevant to the opportunity open to every human being to take a decision to devote his or her entire life to the service of the entire human family. The ancient Jews held that from the illimitable *Ain-Soph* there came a reflection, which could never be more than a partial participation in that illimitable light which transcends manifestation. This reflection exists in the world as archetypal humanity – Adam Kadmon. Every human being belongs to one single humanity, and that collectivity stands in relation to the *Ain-Soph* as any one human being to his or her own father. It is no wonder that Pythagoras – *Pitar Guru*, 'father and teacher,' as he was known among the ancient Hindus – came to Krotona to sound the keynote of a long cycle now being reaffirmed for an equally long period in the future. He taught his disciples to honour their father and their mother, and to take a sacred oath to the Holy Fathers of the human race, the 'Ancestors of the Arhats.'

We are told in the fourth Stanza of *Dzyan* that the Fathers are the Sons of Fire, descended from a primordial host of Logoi. They are self-existing rays streaming forth from a single, central, universal Mahatic fire which is within the cosmic egg, just as differentiated matter is outside and around it. There are seven sub-divisions within Mahat — the cosmic mind, as it was called by the Greeks — as well as seven dimensions of matter outside the egg, giving a total of fourteen planes, fourteen worlds. Where we are told by John that Jesus said, *In my Father's house are many mansions*, H.P. Blavatsky states that this refers to the seven mansions of the central Logos, supremely revered in all religions as the Solar Creative Fire. Any human being who has a true wakefulness and thereby a sincere spirit of obeisance to the divine demiurgic intelligence in the universe, of which he is a trustee even while encased within the lethargic carcass of matter, can show that he is a man to the extent to which he exhibits divine manliness through profound gratitude, a constant recognition and continual awareness of the One Source. All the great Teachers of humanity point to a single source beyond themselves. Many are called but few are chosen by self-election. Spiritual Teachers always point upwards for each and every man and woman alive, not for just a few. They work not only in the visible realm for those immediately before them, but, as John reminds us, they come from above and work for all. They continually think of and love every being that lives and breathes, mirroring "the One that breathes breathless" in ceaseless contemplation, overbrooding the Golden Egg of the universe, the *Hiranyagarbha*.

Such beautiful ideas enshrined in magnificent myths are provocative to the ratiocinative mind and suggestive to the latent divine discernment of Buddhic intuition. The only way anyone can come closer to the Father in Heaven — let alone come closer to Him on earth Who is as He is in Heaven — is by that light to which John refers in the first chapter of the gospel. It is the light that lighteth every man who cometh into the world, which the darkness comprehendeth not. Human beings are involved in the darkness of illusion, of self-forgetfulness, and forgetfulness of their divine ancestry. The whole of humanity may be regarded as a garden of gods but all men and women are fallen angels or gods tarnished by forgetfulness of their true eternal and universal mission. Every man or woman is born for a purpose. Every person has a divine destiny. Every individual has a unique contribution to make, to enrich the lives of others, but no one can say what this is for anyone else. Each one has to find it, first by arousing and kindling and then by sustaining and nourishing the little lamp within the heart. There alone may be lit the true Akashic fire upon the altar in the hidden temple of the God which lives and breathes within. This is the sacred fire of true awareness which enables a man to come closer to the one universal divine consciousness which, in its very brooding upon manifestation, is the father-spirit. In the realm of matter it may be compared to the wind that bloweth where it listeth. Any human being could become a self-conscious and living instrument of that universal divine consciousness of which he, as much as every other man or woman, is an effulgent ray.

This view of man is totally different from that which has, alas, been preached in the name of Jesus. Origen spoke of the constant crucifixion of Jesus, declaring that there is not a day on earth when he is not reviled. But equally there is not a time when others do not speak of him with awe. He came with a divine protection provided by a secret bond which he never revealed except by indirect intonation. Whenever the Logos becomes flesh, there is sacred testimony to the Great Sacrifice and the Great Renunciation — of all Avatars, all Divine Incarnations. This Brotherhood of Blessed Teachers is ever behind every attempt to enlighten human minds, to summon the latent love in human hearts for all humanity, to fan the sparks of true compassion in human beings into the fires of Initiation. The mark of the Avatar is that in him the Paraclete, the Spirit of Eternal Truth, manifests so that even the blind may see, the deaf may hear, the lame may walk, the unregenerate may gain confidence in the possibility and the promise of Self-redemption.

In one of the most beautiful passages penned on this subject, the profound essay entitled "The Roots of Ritualism in Church and Masonry," published in 1889, H.P. Blavatsky declared:

> Most of us believe in the survival of the Spiritual Ego, in Planetary Spirits and *Nirmanakayas*, those great Adepts of the past ages, who, renouncing their right to Nirvana, remain in our spheres of being, not as 'spirits' but as complete spiritual human Beings. Save their corporeal, visible envelope, which they leave behind, they remain as they were, in order to help poor humanity, as far as can be done without sinning against Karmic Law. This is the 'Great

> Renunciation,' indeed; an incessant, conscious self-sacrifice throughout aeons and ages till that day when the eyes of blind mankind will open and, instead of the few, *all* will see the universal truth. These Beings may well be regarded as God and Gods — if they would but allow the fire in our hearts, at the thought of that purest of all sacrifices, to be fanned into the flame of adoration, or the smallest altar in their honour. But they will not. Verily, 'the secret heart is fair Devotion's (only) temple,' and any other, in this case, would be no better than profane ostentation.

Let a man be without external show such as the Pharisees favoured, without inscriptions such as the Scribes specialized in, and without arrogant and ignorant self-destructive denial such as that of the Sadducees. Such a man, whether he be of any religion or none, of whatever race or nation or creed, once he recognizes the existence of a Fraternity of Divine Beings, a Brotherhood of Buddhas, Bodhisattvas and Christs, an Invisible Church (in St. Augustine's phrase) of living human beings ever ready to help any honest and sincere seeker, he will thereafter cherish the discovery within himself. He will guard it with great reticence and grateful reverence, scarcely speaking of his feeling to strangers or even to friends. When he can do this and maintain it, and above all, as John says in the gospel, be true to it and live by it, then he may make it for himself, as Jesus taught, the way, the truth and the light. While he may not be self-manifested as the Logos came to be through Jesus — the Son of God become the Son of Man — he could still sustain and protect himself in times of trial. No man dare ask for more. No man could do with less.

Jesus knew that his own time of trial had come — the time for the consummation of his vision — on the Day of Passover. Philo Judaeus, who was an Aquarian in the Age of Pisces, gave an intellectual interpretation to what other men saw literally, pointing out that the spiritual passover had to do with passing over earthly passions. Jesus, when he knew the hour had come for the completion of his work and the glorification of his father to whom he ever clung, withdrew with the few into the Garden of Gethsemane. He did not choose them, he said. They chose him. He withdrew with them and there they all used the time for true prayer to the God within. Jesus had taught, *Go into thy closet and pray to thy*

father who is in secret, and that, *The Kingdom of God is within you.*
This was the mode of prayer which he revealed and exemplified to
those who were ready for initiation into the Mysteries. Many tried
but only few stayed with it. Even among those few there was a
Peter, who would thrice deny Jesus. There was the traitor, Judas,
who had already left the last supper that evening, having been told,
That thou doest, do quickly. Some among the faithful spent their
time in purification. Were they, at that point, engaged in
self-purification for their own benefit? What had Jesus taught them?
Could one man separate himself from any other? He had told those
who wanted to stone the adulteress, *Let him who is without sin
cast the first stone.* He had told them not to judge anyone else,
but to wait for true judgement. Because they had received a
sublime privilege, about which other men subsequently argued
for centuries and produced myriad heresies and sects, in their case
the judgement involved their compassionate concern to do the
sacred Work of the Father for the sake of all. The Garden of
Gethsemane is always here. It is a place very different from the
Wailing Wall where people gnash their teeth and weep for
themselves or their tribal ancestors. The Garden of Gethsemane is
wherever on earth men and women want to cleanse themselves
for the sake of being more humane in their relations with others.

Nor was the crucifixion only true of Jesus and those two thieves,
one of whom wanted to have a miracle on his behalf while the
other accepted the justice of the law of the day, receiving
punishment for offences that he acknowledged openly. Every man
participates in that crucifixion. This much may be learnt from the
great mystics and inspired poets across two thousand years. Christos
is being daily, hourly, every moment crucified within the cross of
every human being. There are too few on earth who are living up to
the highest possibility of human godlike wisdom, love and
compassion, let alone who can say that in them the spirit of Truth,
the Paraclete, manifests. Who has the courage to chase the
money-changers of petty thoughts and paltry desires from the
Temple of the universal Spirit, not through hatred of the
money-changers, but through a love in his heart for the Restoration
of the Temple? Who has the courage to say openly what all men
recognize inwardly when convenient, or when drunk, or when
among friends whom they think they trust? Who is truly a man?

58

How many men are there heroically suffering? Not only do we know that God is not mocked and that as we sow, so shall we reap, but we also realize that the Garden of Gethsemane is difficult to reach. Nonetheless, it may be sought by any and every person who wants to avoid the dire tragedy of self-annihilation. Indeed, there are many such people all around who barely survive from day to day because of their own self-hatred, self-contempt and despair, and who tremble on the brink of moral death. We live in terribly tragic times, and therefore there is no one who cannot afford to take a little pause for the sake of making the burden of one's presence easier for one's wife or husband, for one's children, or for one's neighbours. Each needs a time of re-examination, a time for true repentance, a time for Christ-like resolve. The Garden of Gethsemane is present wherever there is genuineness, determination and honesty. Above all, it is where there is the joyous recognition that, quite apart from yesterday and tomorrow, right now a person can create so strong a current of thought that it radically affects the future. He could begin now, and acquire in time a self-sustaining momentum. But this cannot be done without overcoming the karmic gravity of all the self-destructive murders of human beings that he has participated in on the plane of thought, on the plane of feeling, especially on the plane of words, and also, indirectly, on the plane of outward action.

If the Garden of Gethsemane did not exist, no persecuting Saul could ever become a Paul. Such is the great hope and the glad tiding. As Origen said, Saul had to be killed before Paul could be born. The Francis who was a simple crusader had to die before the Saint of Assisi could be born. Because all men have free will, no man can transform himself without honest and sincere effort. Hence, after setting out the nature of the Gods, the Fathers of the human race, H.P. Blavatsky, in the same article quoted, spoke of the conditions of probation of incarnated souls seeking resurrection:

> . . . every true Theosophist holds that the divine HIGHER SELF of every mortal man is of the same essence as the essence of these Gods. Being, moreover, endowed with free-will, hence having, more than they, responsibility, we regard the incarnated EGO as far superior to, if not more divine than, any spiritual INTELLIGENCE *still awaiting*

incarnation. Philosophically, the reason for this is obvious, and every metaphysician of the Eastern school will understand it. The incarnated EGO has odds against it which do not exist in the case of a pure divine Essence unconnected with matter; the latter has no personal merit, whereas the former is on his way to final perfection through the trials of existence, of pain and suffering.

It is up to each one to decide whether to make this suffering constructive, these trials meaningful, these tribulations a golden opportunity for self-transformation and spiritual resurrection.

If this decision is not made voluntarily during life, it is thrust upon each ego at death. Every human being has to pass at the moment of death, according to the wisdom of the ancients, to a purgatorial condition in which there is a separation of the immortal individuality. It is like a light which is imprisoned during waking life, a life which is a form of sleep within the serpent coils of matter. This god within is clouded over by the fog of fear, superstition and confusion, and all but the pure in heart obscure the inner light by their demonic deceits and their ignorant denial of the true heart. Every human being needs to cast out this shadow, just as he would throw away an old garment, says Krishna, or just as he would dump into a junkyard an utterly unredeemable vehicle. Any and every human being has to do the same on the psychological plane. Each is in the same position. He has to discard the remnants, but the period for this varies according to each person. This involves what is called 'the mathematics of the soul.' Figures are given to those with ears to hear, and there is a great deal of detailed application to be made.

Was Jesus exempt from this? He wanted no exception. He had taken the cross. He had become one with other men, constantly taking on their limitations, exchanging his finer life-atoms for their gross life-atoms — the concealed thoughts, the unconscious hostilities, the chaotic feelings, the ambivalences, the ambiguities, the limitations of all. He once said, *My virtue has gone out of me,* when the hem of his garment was touched by a woman seeking help, but does this mean that he was exposed only when he physically encountered other human beings? The *Gospel According to John* makes it crisply clear, since it is the most mystical and today the most meaningful of the four gospels, that this was taking place all the time. It not only applies to Jesus. It takes place all the time for every person, often unknown to oneself. But when it is fully self-conscious, the pain is greater, such as when a magnanimous Adept makes a direct descent from his true divine estate, leaving behind his finest elements, like Surya the sun in the myth who cuts off his lustre for the sake of entering into a marriage with Sanjna, coming into the world, and taking on the limitations of all. The Initiator needs the three days in the tomb, but these three days are metaphorical. They refer to what is known in the East as a necessary gestation state when the transformation could be made more smoothly from the discarded vehicle which had been crucified.

People tend to fasten upon the wounds and the blood, even though, as Titian's painting portrays clearly, the tragedy of Jesus was not in the bleeding wounds but in the ignorance and self-limitation of the disciples. He had promised redemption to anyone and everyone who was true to him, which meant, he said, to love each other. He had washed the feet of the disciples, drawn them together, given them every opportunity so that they would do the same for each other. He told them that they need only follow this one commandment. We know how difficult it is for most people today to love one another, to work together, to pull together, to cooperate and not compete, to add and not subtract, to multiply and serve, not divide and rule. This seems very difficult especially in a hypocritical society filled with deceit and lies. What are children to say when their parents ask them to tell the truth and they find themselves surrounded by so many lies? In the current cycle the challenge is most pointed and poignant. More honesty is needed, more courage, more toughness – this time for the sake of all mankind. One cannot leave it to a future moment for some pundits in theological apologetics and theosophical hermeneutics to say this cycle was only for some chosen people. Every single part of the world has to be included and involved.

The teaching of Jesus was a hallowed communication of insights, a series of sacred glimpses, rather than a codification of doctrine. He presented not a *summa theologica* or *ethica*, but the seminal basis from which an endless series of *summae* could be conceived. He initiated a spiritual current of sacred dialogue, individual exploration and communal experiment in the quest for divine wisdom. He taught the beauty of acquiescence and the dignity of acceptance of suffering — a mode appropriate to the Piscean Age. He showed salvation — through love, sacrifice and faith — of the regenerated *psyche* that cleaves to the light of *nous*. He excelled in being all things to all men while remaining utterly true to himself and to his 'Father in Heaven.' He showed a higher respect for the Temple than its own custodians. At the same time he came to found a new kind of kingdom and to bring a message of joy and hope. He came to bear witness to the Kingdom of Heaven during life's probationary ordeal on earth. He vivified by his own luminous sacrifice the universal human possibility of divine self-consecration, the beauty of beatific devotion to the Transcendental Source of Divine Wisdom — the Word Made Flesh celebrating the Verbum In the Beginning.

Above all, there was the central paradox that his mission had to be vindicated by its failure, causing bewilderment among many of his disciples, while intuitively understood only by the very few who were pure in heart and strong in devotion, blessed by the vision of the Ascension. After three days in the tomb, Jesus, in the guise of a gardener, said to a poor, disconsolate Mary Magdalene, *Mary!* At once she looked back because she recognized the voice, and she said, *Rabboni* — "My Master" — and fell at his feet. Then he said, *Touch me not.* Here is a clue to his three days in the tomb. The work of permanent transmutation of life-atoms, of transfiguration of vehicles, was virtually complete. He then said, *Go to my brethren, and say unto them, I ascend unto my Father and your Father; and to my God and your God.* Subsequently he appeared three times to his disciples.

Jesus gave the greatest possible confidence to all his disciples by ever paying them the most sacred compliment, telling them that they were children of God. But, still, if a person thinks that he is nothing, or thinks that he is the greatest sinner on earth, how can the compassion and praise of Jesus have meaning for him? Each person has to begin to see himself undramatically as one of many sinners and say, "My sins are no different from those of anyone else." The flesh is weak but *pneuma*, the spirit, is willing. And *pneuma* has to do with breath. The whole of the *Gospel According to John* is saturated with the elixir of the breathing-in and breathing-out by Jesus of the life-infusing current that gives every man a credible faith in his promise and possibility, and, above all, a living awareness of his immortality, which he can self-consciously realize when freed from mis-identification with his mortal frame.

The possibility of resurrection has to do with identification and mis-identification. This is the issue not for just a few but for all human beings who, in forgetfulness, tend to think that they are what their enemies think, or that they are what their friends want them to be. At one time men talked of the *imago Christi*. We now live in a society that constantly deals in diabolical images and the cynical corruption of image-making, a nefarious practice unfamiliar in simpler societies which still enjoy innocent psychic health. Even more, people now engage in image-crippling — the most heinous of crimes. At one time men did it openly, with misguided courage. They pulled down statues and defaced idols. They paid for it and are still paying. Perhaps those people were reborn in this society. That is sad because they are condemning themselves to something worse than hell — not only the hell of loneliness and despair — but much worse. The light is going out for many a human being. The Mahatmas have always been with us. They have always abundantly sent forth benedictory vibrations. They are here on earth where they have always had their asylums and their ashrams. Under cyclic law they are able to use precisely prepared forums and opportunities to re-erect or resurrect the mystery temples of the future. Thus, at this time, everybody is stirred up by the crucial issue of identity — which involves the choice between the living and the dead, between entelechy and self-destruction.

The central problem in the *Gospel According to John*, which Paul had to confront in giving his sermon on the resurrection, has to do with life and with death. What is life for one man is not life to another. Every man or woman today has to raise the question, "What does it mean for me to be alive, to breathe, to live for the sake of others, to live within the law which protects all but no one in particular?" Whoever truly identifies with the limitless and unconditional love of Jesus and with the secret work of Jesus which he veiled in wordless silence, is lit up. Being lit up, one is able to see the divine Buddha-nature, the light vesture of the Buddha. The disciples in the days of the Buddha, and so again in the days of Jesus, were able to see the divine raiment made of the most homogeneous pure essence of universal *Buddhi.* Immaculately conceived and unbegotten, it is *daiviprakriti*, the light of the Logos. Every man at all times has such a garment, but it is covered over. Therefore, each must sift and select the gold from the dross. The more a person does this truly and honestly, the more the events of what we call life can add up before the moment of death. They can have a beneficent impact upon the mood and the state of mind in which one departs. A person who is wise in this generation will so prepare his meditation that at the moment of death he may read or have read out those passages in the *Bhagavad Gita, The Voice of the Silence,* or the *Gospel According to John* that are exactly relevant to what is needed. Then he will be able to intone the Word, which involves the whole of one's being and breathing, at the moment when he may joyously discard his mortal garment. It has been done, and it is being done. It can be done, and it will be done. Anyone can do it, but in these matters there is no room for chance or deception, for we live in a universe of law. Religion can be supported now by science, and to bring the two together in the psychology of self-transformation one needs true philosophy, the unconditional love of wisdom.

The crucifixion of Jesus and his subsequent resurrection had little reference to himself, any more than any breath he took during his life. Thus, in the gospel we read that Jesus promises that when he will be gone from the world, he will send the Paraclete. This archaic concept has exercised the pens of many scholars. What is the Paraclete? What does it mean? 'Comforter'? 'The Spirit of Truth'? Scholars still do not claim to know. The progress made in this century is in the honest recognition that they do not know, whereas in the nineteenth century they quarrelled, hurled epithets at each other out of arrogance, with a false confidence that did not impress anyone for long. The times have changed, and this is no moment for going back to the pseudo-complacency of scholasticism, because today it would be false, though at one time it might have had some understandable basis. Once it might have seemed a sign of health and could have been a pardonable and protective illusion. Today it would be a sign of sickness because it would involve insulting the intelligence of many young people, men and women, Christian, Jewish,

Protestant, Catholic, but also Buddhist, Hindu, Muslim, Sikh, and every other kind of denomination. No one wants to settle for the absurdities of the past, but all nonetheless want a hope by which they may live and inherit the future, not only for themselves or their descendants, but for all living beings.

This, then, is a moment when people must ask what would comfort the whole of mankind. What did Jesus think would be a way of comforting all? Archetypally, the *Gospel According to John* is speaking in this connection of the mystery temple, where later all the sad failures of Christianity took place. This is the light and the fire that must be kept alive for the sake of all. Who, we may ask, will joyously and silently maintain it intact? Who will be able to say, as the dying Latimer said in Oxford in 1555, "We shall this day light such a candle . . . as I trust shall never be put out." Jesus was confident that among his disciples there were those who had been set afire by the flames that streamed through him. He was the *Hotri*, 'the indispensable agent' for the universal alkahest, the elixir of life and immortality. He was the fig tree that would bear fruit, but he predicted that there would be fig trees that would bear no fruit. He was referring to the churches that have nothing to say, nothing real to offer, and above all, do not care that much for the lost Word or the world's proletariat, or the predicament and destiny of the majority of mankind.

His confidence was that which came to him, like everything in his life, from the Father, the Paraguru, the Lord of Libations, who, with boundless love for all, sustains in secret the eternal contemplation, together with the two Bodhisattvas — one whose eye sweeps over slumbering earth, and the other whose hand is extended in protecting love over the heads of his ascetics. Jesus spoke in the name of the Great Sacrifice. He spoke of the joy in the knowledge that there were a few who had become potentially like the leaven that could lift the whole lump, who had become true Guardians of the Eternal Fires. These are the vestal fires of the mystery temple which had disappeared in Egypt, from which the exodus took place. They had disappeared from Greece, though periodically there were attempts to revive them, such as those by Pythagoras at Delphi. They were then being poured into a new city called Jerusalem. In a sense, the new Comforter was the New

Jerusalem, but it was not just a single city nor was it merely for people of one tribe or race.

Exoterically, the temple of Jerusalem was destroyed in 63 B.C. by Pompey and was rebuilt. Later it was razed to the ground again in 70 A.D. Since the thirteenth century no temple has been in existence there at all because that city has been for these past seven hundred years entirely in the hands of those who razed the old buildings and erected minarets and mosques. Now, people wonder if there really ever was a true Jerusalem, for everywhere is found the Babylon of confusion. Today it is not Origen who speaks to us, but Celsus, on behalf of all Epicureans. Everyone is tempted, like Lot's wife, to be turned into salt by fixing their attention upon the relics and memories of the past long after they have vanished into the limbo of dissolution and decay.

Anyone, however, who has an authentic soul-vision is El Mirador. Jesus knew that the vision, entrusted to the safekeeping of a few, would inspire them to lay the basis of what would continue, because of what they did, despite all the corruption and the ceaseless crucifixion. Even today, two thousand years later, when we hear of the miracle of the limitless love of Jesus, when we hear the words he spoke, when we read about and find comfort in what he did, we are deeply stirred. We are abundantly grateful because in us is lit the chela-light of true reverential devotion to the Christos within. This helps us to see all the Christs of history, unknown as well as renowned, as embodiments of the One and Only — *the One without a Second*, in the cryptic language of the Upanishads. When this revelation takes place and is enjoyed inwardly, there are glad tidings, because it is on the invisible plane that the real work is done. Most people are fixated on the visible and want to wait for fruits from trees planted by other men. There are a few, however, who have realized the comfort to be derived in the true fellowship of those who seek the kingdom of God within themselves, who wish to become the better able to help and teach others, and who will be true in their faith from now until the twenty-first century. Some already have been using a forty-year calendar.

There have been such persons before us. Pythagoras called them Heroes. The Buddha called them *Shravakas*, true listeners, and *Shramanas*, true learners. Then there were some who became *Srotapattis*, 'those who enter the stream,' and among them were a few *Anagamin*, 'those who need never return on earth again involuntarily.' There were also those who were *Arhans* of boundless vision, Perfected Men, Bodhisattvas, endlessly willing to re-enter the cave, having taken the pledge of Kwan-Yin to redeem every human being and all sentient life.

Nothing less than such a vow can resurrect the world today. These times are very different from the world at the time of John because in this age outward forms are going to give no clues in relation to the work of the formless. Mankind has to grow up. We find Origen saying this in the early part of the third century and Philo saying the same even in the first century. Philo, who was a Jewish scholar and a student of Plato, was an intuitive intellectual, while Origen, who had studied the Gnostics and considered various philosophical standpoints, was perhaps more of a mystic or even an ecstatic. Both knew that the Christos could only be seen by the eye of the mind. *If therefore thine eye be single*, Jesus said, *thy whole body shall be full of Light*. Those responding with the eyes of the body could never believe anything because, as Heraclitus said, "Eyes are bad witnesses to the soul." The eyes of the body must be tutored by the eye of the mind. *Gupta Vidya* also speaks of the eye of the heart and the eye in the forehead — the eye of Wisdom-Compassion. Through it, by one's own love, one will know the greater love. By one's own compassion one will know the greater compassion. By one's own ignorance one will recognize the ignorance around and seek the privilege of recognition of the Paraclete. Then, when the eye becomes single in its concentration upon the welfare of all, the body will become full of the light of the Christos. Once unveiled at the fundamental level of causality, it makes a man or woman an eternal witness to the true resurrection of the Son of Man into the highest mansions of the Father.

"The Gospel According to St. John"   RAGHAVAN IYER
Hermes, April 2, 1977

COMPLEMENTARY TEXTS

GNOSTIC THEOGONY

If the *Gospel According to Thomas* contains the oldest compilation of the teachings of Jesus, as some scholars believe, they are nonetheless his secret teachings. The gospels attributed to Matthew and Mark agree that when Jesus taught in public, he taught in parables. Matthew said that the disciples of Jesus wondered about this practice, and Jesus replied: "To you it has been given to know the *mysteria* of the kingdom of heaven, but to them it has not been given" *(Matthew, 13:11). Mysteria* is usually translated 'secrets,' but it literally means 'mysteries.' As the *Gospel According to Thomas* and "The Mystery of Christos" by H.P. Blavatsky make clear, the esoteric teachings were not withheld from the public for élitist reasons: the *mysteria* can be understood only when accompanied by a permanent transformation of consciousness. In Gnostic language, the psychic mind must abandon its obsession with the hylic (material) body and turn ardently towards the pneumatic (spiritual) Light within. Without this fundamental change, the *mysteria* will be mistaken for fantasies, gibberish or hallucinations. Even worse, they may be taken literally and treated as speculative metaphysics, divine biography or philosophical psychology. To the spiritually awakened mind, they are transcendental ontology, theogony and noetic anthropology – in short, *noesis* pointing beyond itself.

Nevertheless, the Gnostic teachings may help those who have not experienced the total reorientation of consciousness, symbolized by the disciples who dropped everything and followed Jesus without hesitation when he called them. H.P. Blavatsky advised open-minded learners to take the subtle teachings of *The Secret Doctrine* as working hypotheses, not just for eventual empirical proof, but as seeds for meditation and contemplation to effect a change in consciousness. The ancient Gnostic teachers put some of their doctrines in writing for the same purpose. Those who knew did not need the recorded texts, and those who were not initiated could not understand them. They could, however, use them to grow in understanding until they came to the threshold of Initiation. The Gnostic gospels and treatises were meant as frameworks to be used in progressive spiritual awakenings. Just as the *Gospel According to Thomas* suggests dimensions and directions of thought reaching far beyond the considerable range found in the orthodox gospels, so other Gnostic scriptures elaborate aspects of the *logia* of Jesus in suggestive ways. Thus they intimate the highest realities and deepest mysteries of the visible and invisible universe.

For early Christians and Gnostics alike, the living heart of the teachings of Jesus centered upon *anastasis,* the resurrection. According to orthodox theology, the resurrection was the conquest of mortality by the Christos. It provided the possibility of human salvation for those who believed in the salvific power of the Christos. In the *Treatise on the Resurrection,* a letter from an unknown Gnostic teacher to a brotherhood of disciples, the resurrection of Jesus is honoured as a path-breaking event. It is not unique in essence, however, but only in time, like the enlightenment of Gautama Buddha. Here the resurrection is nothing less than the pristine, unalterable nature of every human being. The resurrection of Christos is necessary because it exemplifies the pervasive spiritual intelligence without which there could be no life in forms, nor even articulate structure in matter. Recognition of the resurrection in time is the recovery of one's own ultimate nature in an illusory world. It is a revelation rooted in self-knowledge. In everyday practice, this means that one should live as if one has already died (to the world and the flesh) and ascended to heaven. This is the Kingdom of Heaven, treated at length in the *Gospel According to Thomas,* made manifest on earth. To one who knows, theogony is anthropogenesis seen from the standpoint of eternity.

In the opening scene of the *Apocryphon of John,* the enigma of the resurrection indirectly sparks profound questioning by John, the son of Zebedee. The Christos appears to John in a dramatic theophany reminiscent of the appearance of Pymander to Hermes Trismegistus. In elucidating the nature of the descent of the Christos, the scripture sets out an elaborate theogony to explain the fall of humanity and the metaphysical origin of evil. Though cast in mythic terms, it outlines a conception of hierarchies of intelligences which account for the relative unreality of the everyday world, the significance of the struggle between light and darkness, and the possibility of spiritual awakening. Each individual is a fragment of undifferentiated Divine Light imprisoned in differentiating form. Evil is nothing but a crystallization of the good, and since evil is not the opposite of good but rather its radical misappropriation, it is possible for every human being to recover his original spiritual freedom, which is immortality.

While a few belong to the Immovable Race by virtue of their immediate recognition of the Christos, that is, of incarnate Light and Truth, most will understand only by stages. They will have to reincarnate again and again until they are purified sufficiently in consciousness to join the perfected men who live in the Divine Light. The resurrection of Man and the redemption of the world is truly a restoration of consciousness to its primordial Wisdom — the veil which hides the "Pure Light which no eye can behold." This theophanous redemptive process is akin to *tikkun*, restoration, as found in the Zoharic Kabbalah and elaborated by Isaac Luria and the Safed Kabbalists. It is the release of imprisoned Light by the universal radiation of the Spiritual Sun focussed in the descending Logos.

The *Treatise on the Resurrection* appears to belong to a broad and diverse cluster of schools which looked to the great Gnostic teacher Valentinos as their founder. The *Evangelium Veritatis* may have been dictated by Valentinos himself, as a few scholars believe. In the *Gospel of Truth* theogony becomes transcendental psychology, for the descent of the Logos is the revelation of the Name. The emancipating reversal of consciousness is effected by the discovery of one's real name. The Christos, who is the Name of the Unnameable, descends as a Light consubstantial with the imprisoned Light that constitutes the essence of every human being. Man discovers the greater Light by releasing the Light within himself. This epiphany is epistemic, for evil, corruption, delusion and confusion are the result of ignorance *(agnosis)*, a deficiency of unbound Light. Freedom consists in self-knowledge, a discovery of one's name (that is, real immortal nature) through hearing the teaching of the Name, who is the Christos. Self-knowledge leads to — and in fact is identical with — knowledge of the Father, because all human beings are sons of God. *Gnosis* is, therefore, knowledge of the Name. This spiritual knowledge is Truth, and its ontic correlate in consciousness is indescribable joy, the unconditional bliss which is the afflatus of the Unnameable, the *ananda* of Hindu and Buddhist traditions.

According to ancient Christian legend, when the disciples were charged by Jesus to go forth into the world and preach, they wavered for a time, not knowing what to do. But the descent of the Holy Spirit upon them, represented by a divine fire blazing over their heads and celebrated in Pentecost, made all things clear. Each disciple, the legend declares, went to a different quarter of the earth to spread the gospel, the 'good news.' Given the remarkable status Jesus conferred on Judas Thomas in *logion* 13 of the *Gospel According to Thomas,* it is not surprising that he journeyed to India, home of Sages and Initiates and putative abode of the resurrected Jesus. The *Acts of Thomas,* a non-canonical text long known in Christendom, deals with his work there. A short passage in the *Acta Thomae* stands on its own as a classic spiritual statement. Called *Song of the Pearl,* it is a poetic elucidation of the Gnostic doctrine of the descent, imprisonment and restoration of the soul. In the poem, the Orient (India) represents the immutable spiritual realm and Egypt (the Occident) the material world of incarnated existence. The "imprisoned splendour," the Light trapped in form, is depicted as a pearl surrounded by a hideous dragon. The sojourner is the *pneuma,* the pearl the *psyche,* and the dragon, the powers of material nature.

The spiritual pilgrim has to lay aside his celestial vestures — the formless essences which manifest in the differentiated world as forces and powers — and descend through planes of increasing differentiation and fragmentation. He takes on Egyptian clothes (flesh), partakes of Egypt's food, and soon forgets his real nature and mission. His parents, his spiritual Source and Root, send him a reminder and he awakens from his torpor, rescues the pearl and reascends to his true abode. The *Song of the Pearl* equates theogony with noetic anthropology. As theogony, it describes the descent of the Christos-Logos, his Father's call (reminiscent of the descent of the dove when Jesus was baptized by John), and his reascent with the spiritually awakened human soul. As the story of man, it tells the tale of incarnation, the appearance of the Logos (in the form of a letter) as consubstantial with the human heart, and the joyous reascent of consciousness to its original home.

These sacred texts were composed by different authors at different times, though all before 150 A.D. The *Treatise on the*

Resurrection and the *Evangelium Veritatis* survive in Subachmimic (a language very close to Coptic), the *Apocryphon of John* in Coptic, and the *Song of the Pearl* in Syriac. Whatever their divergences in detail, they share in common the central themes of the *Gospel According to Thomas.* Man is divine in origin, nature and ultimate destiny. Jesus, who realized the Christos-Light in himself, taught all who would listen that the Light is within each one. The human being and the highest manifest deity are one in ultimate essence, and both as a sempiternal Unity constitute the luminous veil over the unknowable Absolute. Since the incarnated individual experiences temporally, the cosmic architectonics of Light, Life and Logos is reflected as an historical and spiritual unfoldment in man. For the Gnostic, the message of Jesus is that each human being may theurgically reverse the descent of the soul and the ascent of the Christos. In this way the Kingdom of Heaven, which is always necessarily 'at hand,' is manifest on earth, and humanity realizes in consciousness its spiritual nature. Theogony exists for theophany, and theophany for true, eternal redemption, rescuing the immortal element in Man and elevating Nature to become a more perfect vehicle for the Light of the Logos.

ELTON HALL

TREATISE ON THE RESURRECTION

There are some, Rheginos my son, who desire to learn much. This is their goal when they are concerned with questions the answers to which are lacking. If they taste success, they usually think highly of themselves. Yet I do not think that they take their stand in the Word of Truth. Rather, they seek their own repose, which we have received through our Soter, our Lord Christos. We were given repose when we knew the Truth and established ourselves in it. Since, however, you courteously inquire of us the meaning of the resurrection *(anastasis)*, I am writing to say that it is necessary. Verily, multitudes lack faith in it; nonetheless, a few find it. So let us take up the subject.

How did the Lord conduct himself during his existence in the flesh and after he had manifested as the Son of God? He abided in this place where you abide, speaking of the Law of Nature. I, however, call it Death. Now, Rheginos, the Son of God was the Son of Man. He embraced both divinity and humanity, so that he might vanquish death through being Son of God, and he might effect restoration to the *pleroma* through being Son of Man. He was a seed of the Truth, originally from above, before the cosmic structure had come into being. Within this structure, myriad dominions and divinities came into manifestation.

I know that I am offering the solution in difficult terms, though there is nothing difficult in the Word of Truth. Since the Solution appeared to reveal openly all things and leave nothing hidden — the annihilation of evil on the one side, the revelation of the elect on the other — this is the emanation of Truth and Spirit. Grace belongs to Truth.

The Soter swallowed death — as you well know — for he laid aside the perishable world. He transformed himself into an imperishable *aeon* and raised himself up. Having swallowed the visible by the invisible, he showed us the way of immortality. Therefore, in the words of the Apostle,* "We suffered with him, and we arose with him, and we went to heaven with him." Now,

* "The Apostle" refers to Paul; compare *Romans*, 8:17, and *Ephesians*, 2:5-6.

since we are manifest in the world clothed in him and we are his rays, we are embraced by him until our setting, which is to say, until our death in this life. We are gathered to heaven by him like rays by the sun: this is the spiritual resurrection which swallows up the psychic in the same way as the corporeal.

Nonetheless, if one has no faith, he cannot be persuaded. For this is from the standpoint of faith, my son, and not from that of argumentation: the dead shall arise. If there is even one among the philosophers who has this faith, at least he will arise. But let no philosopher bound to his world believe that he will return on his own. Rather, it is because of our faith. We have known the Son of Man and have faith that he rose from among the dead. This is he of whom we affirm: "He became the destruction of death, for he is a Great One in whom they believe." Great, therefore, are those who have faith.

The thinking of those who are redeemed is imperishable. The consciousness of those who have known him shall not perish. We are elected to salvation and redemption, even predestined from the beginning to shun the foolishness of the ignorant. We shall enter the Wisdom of those who know the Truth. Verily, the Truth which is guarded cannot be abandoned — and it has not been. "Strong is the system of the *pleroma,* and minute is that which fell away and became the world. The All is wholly encompassed. It has not come into being; it ever exists."

Have no doubts about the resurrection, Rheginos my son. If you once were without flesh, you nonetheless received a body when you entered this world. Why then would you have no form when you ascend into the *aeon*? That which is superior to flesh, which came into being for your sake and is, in fact, the cause of life, is not that yours? And does not that which is yours already exist with you? Yet, while you tarry in the world, what is it that you lack? This is what you have been striving to learn.

The afterbirth of the body is old age, and so you dwell in corruption. You have absence as a gain. You will not sacrifice what is superior when you depart. What is worse grows less, but there is grace even for it.

Nothing, then, redeems us from this world save the All which we actually are: thus are we redeemed. We have received salvation from end to end. Let us think in this way! Let us understand in this way!

Yet there are some who make inquiry in order to understand whether one who is redeemed is saved immediately upon departure from the body. There is no need for doubt: the visible aspects which are dead will never be saved, but the living aspects which exist within arise.

Then what is the resurrection? It is the unveiling of the ascended. You remember reading in the gospel* that Elijah appeared with Moses, so do not think the resurrection is an illusion. Rather than an illusion, it is Truth. It is more accurate to say that the world is an illusion in comparison with the resurrection which came into being through our Lord Soter, Jesus the Christos.

But what am I saying? The living shall die. How do they live in an illusion? The rich become poor and kings are dethroned. Everything is subject to change. The world is an illusion, but I must take care not to rail at things to excess.

This is the nature of the resurrection, for it is the Truth which remains firm. It is the revelation of what is, the transformation of things, a transition into newness. Imperishability enters the perishable. Light flows down upon darkness and swallows it. The *pleroma* fills deficiency. These are the symbols and images of the resurrection. It makes the Good.

Therefore, O Rheginos, do not think fragmentarily nor live in accordance with this flesh for the sake of conformity. Flee, rather, from the divisions and the fetters, and thereby you have at hand the resurrection. If one who will die knows that he will eventually die, he is brought to this even though he spends many years in this life. So why not consider yourself as already risen and brought to this? If you are possessed of the resurrection yet live as if you are to die, even though you know you have died already, why should you ignore exercise? It is right for each individual to practise in a number of ways, for he will find release from this Element and will not go astray. He will receive again what he first was.

All this I have gained through the magnanimity of my Lord Jesus Christos. I have taught you and your brothers, all my sons, and I left out nothing that might give you strength. If anything remains obscure in my explanation of the Word, I shall interpret it

---

* The gospel passage is *Mark*, 9:2-8.

whenever you ask. But do not be envious of anyone among you who is able to help.

Many are looking forward to what I have written to you. To them I say: peace and grace. I greet you and those who cherish you in brotherly love.

Treatise on the Resurrection

APOCRYPHON OF JOHN

This is the teaching of the Mysteries, the things hidden in Silence, which the Soter taught John, his disciple.

It happened one day when John, the brother of James — who are both the sons of Zebedee — went up and came to the temple, that a Pharisee named Arimanius approached him and asked, "Where is your Master whom you followed?"

John answered, "He has returned to the place whence he came."

Then the Pharisee said to him, "This Nazarene misled all of you with a deception, filling your minds with falsehoods, closing your hearts and estranging you from the traditions of your fathers."

When I heard these things, I turned away from the temple to a solitary mountain, and with great grief I thought in my heart, "How was the Soter anointed, and why was he sent by his Father? Who is the Father, and what is that Aeon to which we shall go? For what did he mean when he said, 'This Aeon is of the impress of the imperishable Aeon,' although he did not teach us about the archetypal Aeon?"

Even while thinking this, behold, the heavens opened, creation under heaven shone, and the world was shaken. I was frightened, and I saw in the light a youth by me. While I gazed, he appeared as an old man. And he altered again, becoming like a servant. There was no multiplicity before me, but there was a similitude of many forms in the light, and the forms appeared to pass through one another, and the likeness had three forms.

He said to me, "John, John, why do you doubt, and why are you afraid? Are you not familiar with this likeness? Do not fear. I am the one who is with you forever. I am the Father, I am the Mother, I am the Son. I am the Unmixed One and the Incorruptible One. Now I have come to show you what is, what was, and what will come to be, so that you might understand the unmanifest and the manifest, and to teach you about the Perfect Man. Now, lift up your countenance, so that you may receive the things I shall tell you today, that you may in turn instruct your Homopneumata,*

* *Homopneumata*, like spirits, fellow spirits, from *homo*, same, and *pneuma*, breath of spirit.

who are of the Indomitable Race of the Perfect Man."

He knew what I sought to learn and this is what he said to me: The Monad is sovereignty with nothing above it. It is that which exists as Lord and Father of all things, who is beyond imperishability, abiding as Pure Light which no eye can behold. He is the Invisible. It is wrong to think of him as a god or something like it, for he is more than a god, since there is none above him, nor does anyone reign over him. He abides in nothing inferior — all things exist in him. Yet he stands alone, because he has need of nothing. He is utterly perfect and never lacked anything to be completed. He is completely perfect in himself. He is without limit because there is nothing to limit him. He is beyond investigation because there is no one to examine him. He is immeasurable because no one can set the standard. He is invisible because none ever saw him. He is eternal, having never not existed. He is ineffable because none can comprehend him to speak about him. He is unnameable because none can give him a name.

This is the Immeasurable Light, holy and pure. He is ineffable in imperishability, but not in perfection, beatitude or divinity, since he utterly transcends these. He is neither corporeal nor incorporeal. He is neither great nor small. One cannot ask, "What is his quantity?" or "What is his quality?", for none can know him. He surpasses all that exists, not as if he were superior in rank, but because his essence belongs neither to the Aeons nor to time. Whatever belongs to an Aeon was formed. Time was not allotted to him, for he receives naught from another. What is received is a loan, and he who exists prior to someone has no need to be fulfilled by that one. Rather, that one looks up expectantly to him in his Light.

He is majestic; he is pure and limitless Infinitude. He is the Eternal who grants eternity, the life-giving Life, the Blessed who bestows blessedness, the Good who gives goodness, the redemptive Mercy who offers mercy, the Grace who gives grace, not because he possesses it but because he radiates immeasurable and incomprehensible Light.

How shall I tell you about him? His Aeon is immutable and abides in Repose, being in Silence prior to all things. He is chief of all Aeons, and he sustains them through his goodness. We know neither finite nor immeasurable things save for him who emanated from the Father. He alone taught it to us, and he alone looks at him through the afflatus of his Light. This is the spring of the water of life which pours forth in all the Aeons and in every form. He sees his image in the spring of Pneuma and infuses with his desire the Light-water which is the spring of transparent Light-water surrounding him.

And his Ennoia,* thought, who had appeared to him in the nebula of his Light, came forth and acted. This is the primal power which was before the All and which emanated from his Mind, the Pronoia,† forethought, of the All. Her light is the image of the Light, the perfect power which is the portrait of the Invisible Pristine Spirit who is perfect. The primal power, Barbelo,‡ the supreme glory in the Aeons and the glory of the revelation, extolled and glorified the virginal Spirit, for because of him she had manifested. This is the first Ennoia, the image of the Father, who became the Archetypal Man, the holy Pneuma, the thrice-male, the thrice-powerful, the thrice-named Androgyne, the eternal Aeon among the invisible Aeons, and the first to come forth.

Barbelo petitioned the Invisible Pristine Spirit to grant her Prognosis, foreknowledge, and the Spirit consented. And upon his consent Prognosis came forth and stood by the Pronoia. Its origin is the thought of the Invisible Pristine Spirit. It glorified him and Barbelo, his perfect power, for due to her it had come forth.

Again Barbelo petitioned the Spirit to give her Aphtharsia,§ imperishability, and he consented. And upon his consent, Aphtharsia came forth and stood by Ennoia and Prognosis. It glorified the Invisible One and Barbelo, for due to her it had come forth.

And again Barbelo petitioned the Spirit to send her Aionia Zoe, eternal life, and he consented. And upon his consent, Aionia Zoe came forth, and they stood together and glorified the Invisible

* *Ennoia,* thought, concept.

† *Pronoia,* forethought, Providence, conception.

‡ The personified *Shekinah* or Divine Presence.

§ *Aphtharsia,* imperishability, indestructibility.

One and Barbelo, for due to her they had come forth.

Once more Barbelo petitioned the Spirit for Aletheia, truth, and the Invisible Spirit consented. Aletheia came forth and they stood together and glorified the Invisible Perfect Spirit and his Barbelo, due to whom they had manifested.

This is Pentas,* the Five Aeons of the Father: it is the Archetypal Man, the image of the Invisible Spirit; it is Pronoia which is Barbelo, Ennoia and Prognosis, Aphtharsia, Aionia Zoe and Aletheia. This is the Androgyne Pentas which is Dekas,† the Ten Aeons in one, which is the Father.

The Father gazed on Barbelo with the virgin Light that is the afflatus of the Invisible Spirit and with his spark, and she was fructified. He begot a luminous spark with a light of blessed likeness, but it does not equal his greatness. This was Monogenes, the only begotten one, of the Mother-Father which had come into being. It is his only begotten, Autogenetos, self-begotten, of the Father who is Pure Light.

The Invisible Pristine Spirit rejoiced over the emanated Light which emerged and was brought forth by Barbelo, the first power of his Pronoia. He anointed it with his goodness until it became perfect, not lacking in good because he had saturated it with the goodness of the Invisible Spirit. It stood before him and he showered good upon it. At once upon receiving good from the Spirit, it glorified the Pristine Spirit and the unblemished Pronoia and Barbelo, due to whom it had come forth.

It petitioned the Spirit to be given a companion worker, which is Nous,‡ mind, and he consented. Upon the consent of the Invisible Spirit, Nous came forth. It stood by Christos glorifying him and Barbelo.

All these came into being in Silence and Anoia, want of understanding.

And Nous wished to act through the Logos§ of the Invisible Spirit. His will became deed and appeared beside Nous, and the

* *Pentas*, fifth.

† *Dekas*, tenth.

‡ *Nous*, mind, intellect.

§ *Logos*, word, cause, reason.

Light glorified it. The Logos followed the Will. Because of the Logos, Christos, the divine Autogenes,* created all things. Aionia Zoe, his Will and Nous, and Prognosis stood together and glorified the Invisible Spirit and Barbelo, due to whom they had come forth.

And the Holy Spirit completed the divine Autogenes, his son together with Barbelo, that he might stand before the mighty Invisible Pristine Spirit as the divine Autogenes, the Christos, whom he honoured with a powerful voice. He emanated through Pronoia, and the Invisible Pristine Spirit established the divine Autogenes of Truth over all things. To him was subjected every authority and even the Truth within him, so that he might know the All which has been named with a name exalted above all others, a name told only to those worthy of it.

Out of the Light which is Christos, from the divine Autogenes and from Aphtharsia, through the gift of the Spirit, he looked out so that they might take stations by him. The three are Will, Ennoia and Aionia Zoe. But the four powers are Synesis† (insight), Charis (grace), Aisthesis (perception) and Phronesis (prudence).

Charis dwells with Armozel, the Aeon of Light who is the first angel. Three other Aeons abide with this Aeon — Charis, Aletheia and Morphe (form).

The Second Light is Oroiel, who has the station of the second Aeon, accompanied by three additional Aeons — Pronoia, Aisthesis and Memory.

The Third Light is Daveithai, who rules the third Aeon, accompanied by three other Aeons — Synesis, Agape‡ (love) and Idea.

The fourth Aeon is governed by Eleleth, the Fourth Light, accompanied by three Aeons — Perfection, Eirene (peace) and Sophia (wisdom).

These are the four Lights which stand by the divine Autogenes, and these are the twelve Aeons which stand by Autogenes-Christos, the son of the Mighty One, through the will and the gift of the

---

* *Autogenes = Autogenetos*, self-begotten.

† *Synesis*, insight, understanding.

‡ *Agape*, love, fellowship.

Invisible Spirit. The twelve Aeons belong to Autogenes, the son, and all things have been founded by the will of the Holy Spirit through the Autogenes.

The Perfect Man, the first revelation and the Truth, emerged from Prognosis and the perfect Nous through the revelation of the will of the Invisible Spirit and the will of the Autogenes. The Pristine Spirit called him Pigeraadamas and placed him on the first Aeon with the mighty Autogenes-Christos amidst the First Light, Armozel. His powers are with him. The Invisible One gave him an invincible and intelligible power, and he glorified and exalted the Invisible Spirit with the words: "Because of thee all things have come into being, and all things will return to thee. I shall exalt and glorify thee and the Autogenes and the Aeons — the Three: the Father, the Mother and the Son, the perfect power."*

Pigeraadamas put his son Seth on the second Aeon amidst the Second Light, Oroiel. In the third Aeon, amidst the Third Light, Daveithai, the seed of Seth was placed along with the souls of the saints. In the fourth Aeon were placed the souls of those ignorant of the Pleroma who did not repent at once, but who spent a while before repenting. They are in the Fourth Light, Eleleth. They glorify the Invisible Spirit.

The Sophia of the Epinoia,† being an Aeon, conceived a thought from herself with the reflection of the Invisible Spirit and Prognosis. She desired to emanate an image from herself without the consent of the Spirit, for he had not approved, and without the agreement of her consort. Although her male aspect had not approved, and though she had found no agreement, and though she had thought without the consent of the Spirit, nonetheless she brought forth. Since the invisible power is within her, her thought could not be barren, and so an imperfect thing came out of her, differing from her in appearance because she had emanated it without her consort. It was unlike its mother and had another form.

When she beheld the results of her desire, it had assumed the form of a serpent with the countenance of a lion. Its flashing eyes were like fires. She cast it away from her outside that place so that

* The three refer to the Invisible Pristine Spirit (the Father), Autogenes-Christos (the Son) and the Aeons (collectively, the Aeon who is Barbelo, the Mother).

† *Epinoia,* thinking upon, purposive thought.

none of the Immortal Ones might see it, for she had given birth to it in Agnoia, ignorance. She confined it in a cloud of light and she placed a throne in the centre of the cloud so that none might see it save the Holy Spirit, who is Zoe, the mother of all. Then she named him Ialdabaoth. This is the First Archon, who seized enormous power from his mother and fled her, abandoning the place where he was born.

He grew mighty and created for himself other Aeons with flames of shimmering fire in which he still dwells. He joined with the Unreason which is in him and fostered powers for himself. The name of the first is Athoth, and the second is Harmes, the eye of envy. The third is Kalila-Oumbri and the fourth Iabel. The fifth is Adonaiou, who is called Sabaoth, and the sixth is Cain, whom the generations of men call the sun. The seventh is Abel, the eighth Abrisene, the ninth Iobel, the tenth Armoupieel and the eleventh Melcheir-Adonein. The twelfth is Belias, who presides over the abyss of Hades. He placed seven kings, one for each firmament, over the seven heavens and five kings over the depth of the abyss, so that they might reign. He shared his fire with them, but he did not emanate the power of his mother's light which he had seized, for he is the Ignorant Darkness.

When the Light commingled with the darkness, it caused the darkness to shine, but when the darkness mixed with the Light, it dimmed the Light, which became neither bright nor dark but rather weak.

Now the Archon who is weak has three names. The first is Ialdabaoth, the second is Saklas and the third is Samael. He is unholy in his Unreason which dwells in him, for he said, "I am God and there is no other God beside me." He is ignorant of his true strength, which is the place from which he came.

The Archons created seven powers for themselves and the powers created for themselves six angels for each one until they became three hundred and sixty-five angels. These are the corporeal forms belonging with the names: first of all, Athoth, whose face is that of a sheep; secondly, Eloaiou, whose face is that of a donkey; thirdly, Astaphaios with the face of a hyena; fourthly, Iao, whose face is a seven-headed serpent; fifthly, Sabaoth with the dragon-face; sixthly, Adonein, whose face is that of a monkey; and seventhly, Sabbede, whose face is shining fire. This is the Hebdomas of the week.

But Ialdabaoth has a myriad faces in addition to these so that he can manifest a face according to his desire, being in the middle of the seraphs. He shared his fire with them and thereby became lord over them through the power of the glory he possessed of his mother's Light. So he called himself God. Since he did not put his trust in the place whence he came, he merged with the seven powers through his thought. He named each power beginning with the highest, and as he spoke it happened. The first is goodness with the first Archon, Athoth; the second is foreknowledge with the second Archon, Eloaiou; the third is divinity with Astaphaios, the fourth is lordship with Iao; the fifth is kingdom with Sabaoth, the sixth is envy with Adonein; and the seventh is understanding with Sabbateon. Each of these have a firmament which corresponds to an Aeon-heaven. They were named according to the heaven for the powers. There was power in the names given them by their Originator, but the names given them in accordance with the glory that belongs to Heaven mean destruction and powerlessness for them. So they have two names.

He ordered everything after the paradigm of the first extant Aeons so that he might create them to resemble the Imperishable Ones. He had not seen the Imperishable Ones, of course; nonetheless, the power in him which he usurped from his mother produced in him the likeness of the cosmos. When he beheld the creation surrounding him and the angelic multitude which came forth from and encompassed him, he said: "I am a jealous God and there is no God beside me." Yet in so saying, he intimated to the angels who attended him that another God exists. For if there were none other, of whom would he be jealous?

Then the mother began to hover. She knew the deficiency when her brilliant Light dimmed. She became dark because her consort had not consented.

And I said: Lord, what does "she hovered" mean?

He smiled and said: Do not think it is, as Moses wrote, "above the waters."* Not at all, for when she beheld the wickedness which had befallen and her son's thievery, she repented.

---

* This is a reference to *Genesis,* 1:2, where the Spirit is said to hover (to move to and fro) over the Deep.

86

Forgetfulness overwhelmed her in the darkness of Ignorance and she felt shame. So she moved about, though she did not dare to return. This moving is hovering. The Arrogant One stole power from his mother, but he was ignorant, thinking that none other existed save his mother. When he saw the angels of his creation, he felt exalted over them.

Seeing that the plane of darkness was imperfect, the mother knew that her consort had not consented, and she repented with flowing tears. The whole Pleroma heard her prayer of repentance and petitioned on her behalf the Invisible Pure Spirit. He consented and the Holy Spirit poured its fullness over her. Although her consort had not come to her, he descended to her through the Pleroma so that he might correct her deficiency. She was not taken up into her own Aeon; rather, she was set above her son, abiding in the Enneas, the Ninth, until she had corrected her lack.

And a voice issued from the sublime Aeon-heaven: "Man exists and the Son of Man." Ialdabaoth, the chief Archon, heard the voice and thought that it came from his mother, but he knew not where she was. The holy Mother-Father instructed them in the perfect undiminished Prognosis (the image of the Invisible One who is the Father of the Pleroma through whom everything came into existence), the first Man, his appearance in human form.

And the entire Aeon of the chief Archon shook, and the foundations of the abyss trembled. The underside of the waters above the material world was illuminated by the appearance of his revealed image. When the chief Archon and all his authorities looked up, they beheld the form of the image in the water.

And Ialdabaoth said to his attendant authorities, "Come, let us form a man according to the image of God and resembling our likeness, so that his image may be a light for us." They created from one another's powers along the lines indicated. Each authority furnished a characteristic reflecting that aspect of the image which he had beheld in its psychic form. Thus Ialdabaoth created a being resembling the first, perfect Man. And they said, "Let us call him Adam that his name may become the power of light for us."*

So the powers began: first of all goodness created the osseous soul, then foreknowledge created the sinewy soul. The third,

* *Adam* means 'man' in Hebrew.

divinity, formed the fleshly soul, and the fourth, lordship, produced the marrow soul. The fifth, kingdom, created the sanguineous soul, while envy engendered the dermal soul. The seventh, understanding, formed the eyelid soul. And the angelic host stood around him and gathered the powers of the seven substances of the psychic form in order to create each of the parts. The first one began to create the head:

> Eteraphope-Abron formed the head;
> Meniggesstroeth created the brain;
> Asterechme the right eye and Thaspomocha the left eye;
> Yeronumos the right ear and Bissoum the left;
> Akioreim the nose;
> Banen-Ephroum the lips;
> Amen the teeth and Ibikan the molars;
> Basiliademe the tonsils and Achchan the uvula;
> Adaban the neck and Chaaman the vertebrae;
> Dearcho the throat;
> Tebar the shoulder;
> Mniarchon the elbow;
> Abitrion the right underarm and Evanthen the left underarm;
> Krys the right hand and Beluai the left hand;
> Treneu the right fingers and Balbel the left;
> Kriman the fingernails;
> Astrops the right breast and Barroph the left;
> Baoum the right shoulder joint and Ararim the left;
> Areche the belly;
> Phthave the navel;
> Senaphim the abdomen;
> Arachethopi the right ribs and Zabedo the left;
> Barias the right hip and Phnouth the left;
> Abenlenarche the marrow;
> Chnoumeninorin the bones;
> Gesole the stomach;
> Agromauma the heart;
> Bano the lungs;
> Sostrapal the liver;
> Anesimalar the spleen;
> Thopithro the intestines;
> Biblo the kidneys;
> Roeror the sinews;
> Taphreo the spine;

Ipouspoboba the veins and Bineborin the arteries;
The breath of Atoimenpsephei suffuses the limbs, and
Enthollein all the flesh;
Bedouk the womb;
Arabeei the penis;
Eilo the testes;
Sorma the genitalia;
Gormakaiochlabar the right thigh and Nebrith the left;
Pserem the lymph of the right leg and Asaklas that of the left;
Ormaoth the right leg and Emenum the left;
Knyx the right shin and Tupelon the left;
Achiel the right knee and Phneme the left;
Phiouthrom the right foot and Boabel its toes;
Trachoun the left foot and Phikna its toes; and
Miamai the toenails.

And presiding powers were appointed over all of these — Zathoth, Kalila and Yabel and those who operate specifically in the limbs:

Diolimodraza in the head;
Yammeax in the neck;
Yakouib in the left shoulder and Verton in the right;
Oudidi in the right hand and Arbao in the left;
Lampno in the right fingers and Leekaphar in the left;
Barbar in the right breast and Imae in the left;
Pisandriaptes in the chest;
Koade in the right shoulder and Odeor in the left;
Asphixix in the right ribs and Synogchouta in the left;
Arouph in the belly;
Sabalo in the womb;
Charcharb in the right thigh and Chthaon in the left;
Bathinoth in the genitalia;
Choox in the right leg and Charcha in the left;
Aroer in the right shin and Toechea in the left;
Aol in the right knee and Charaner in the left;
Bastan in the right foot and Archentechtha in its toes;
Marephnounth in the left foot and Abrana in its toes.

Seven presided over all of these, and they are Michael, Ouriel, Asmenedas, Saphasatoel, Aarmouriam, Richram and Amiorps. He who rules over the senses is Archendekta. Deitharbathas governs receptivity, while Oummaa guides the imagination. The composition is ruled by Aachiaram and the governor of the entire impulse is Riaramnacho.

There are four sources for the demons that abide in the body — heat, cold, wetness and dryness — but the mother of them all is matter. Heat is ruled by Phloxopha, and Oroorrothos reigns over coldness. Dryness is the realm of Erimacho and wetness belongs to Athuro. The mother of all these has placed Onorthochras in their midst because she is illimitable and mixes with all of them. She is truly matter, for all of these are nourished through her.

The four cardinal demons are Ephememphi, who governs pleasure, Yoko, who rules desire, Nenentophni, governor of grief, and Blaomen, king of fear. Their mother is Aesthesis-Ouchepiptoe. These four demons emanate the passions. Grief produces envy, jealousy, distress, trouble, pain, callousness, anxiety, mourning and all of that kind. Pleasure engenders much wickedness as well as empty pride and similar passions. Desire fosters anger, wrath, bitterness, cruel passions, insatiability and all their kin. Fear gives rise to dread, fawning, agony and shame. While these resemble useful as well as evil things, insight into their true nature is Anaro, the head of the material soul, for she belongs with Ouchepiptoe, the seven senses.

The number of angels is together three hundred and sixty-five. They all laboured on the psychic and material body until they completed it. There are other regents over the remaining passions, but I will not discuss them. If you wish to know them, they are in the *Book of Zoroaster*. All these angels and demons worked until they had constructed the psychic body. But their production was utterly inactive and without motion for a long time.

Then the mother desired to retrieve the power she had yielded to the chief Archon. She petitioned the most merciful Mother-Father of the All. Through a holy decree, he sent the five lights down to the abode of the angels of the chief Archon. They counselled him to bring forth the power of the mother, saying to Ialdabaoth: "Blow into his face a portion of your spirit, which is the power of his mother, and his body will arise." And Ialdabaoth breathed into his face the spirit which is the mother's power, but his ignorance prevented him from knowing this. So the power of the mother went out of Ialdabaoth and entered the psychic soul which they had fashioned in the image of the One who ever exists.

The body moved and gained strength, and it was luminous.

In that moment the other powers became jealous, for he had come into existence through all of them. They had given their power to the man, and his intelligence surpassed that of his makers and even that of the chief Archon. When they beheld his luminosity, his superior thought and his freedom from wickedness, they seized him and threw him into the lowest region of matter.

Then the Blessed One, the Mother-Father, who is beneficent and merciful, had compassion for the mother's power now released from the chief Archon, for the Archons might regain power over the psychic and perceptible body. The One dispatched, through his beneficent Spirit and great mercy, luminous Epinoia, who comes from him and is called Life, as a helper to Adam. She aids the whole creature, working with him, restoring him to his fullness, teaching him about the descent of his seed and instructing him in the path of ascent — which is the same as that by which he descended. Luminous Epinoia was secreted away in Adam so that the Archons would not know her, and so that Epinoia could help correct the deficiency of the mother.

And man emerged through the reflection of the light within him. His thinking was superior to all his makers, and when they beheld him they knew it. They took counsel with the entire company of Archons and angels, and they mixed fire and earth and water with the four fiery winds. They fused them together and created a great disturbance. They drew Adam into the shadow of death to form him anew from earth, water and fire and from the spirit whose origin is matter, that is, the ignorance of darkness and desire, and from the contrary spirit which is the sepulchre of the newly formed body. The thieves clothed the man in this body, which is the bond of forgetfulness. Thus he became a mortal man.

This is the one who descended and the first separation. But luminous Epinoia was in him, and she will awaken his thinking.

Then the Archons set Adam in paradise, saying to him: "Eat at leisure." Their luxury is bitter and their beauty depraved. Their luxury deceives, for their trees are godlessness, their fruit deadly poison and their promise death. They placed the tree of their life in the centre of the garden.

What they call the Tree of Knowledge of Good and Evil is the luminous Epinoia, and they surrounded it so that Adam might not look upon his fullness and comprehend the nakedness of his shamefulness. Nonetheless, I brought it about that they ate of the tree.

And I said to the Soter: "Lord, did not the serpent teach Adam to eat?"

The Soter smiled and said: The serpent taught them to eat of wickedness, begetting lust and destruction, so that Adam might be useful to him. But because of the light of Epinoia within him, Adam knew that he was disobedient to the chief Archon, for Epinoia corrected his thinking so that it surpassed that of the chief Archon. The Archon wanted to withdraw the power he himself had given Adam, so he brought forgetfulness upon him.

And I asked the Soter: "What is this forgetfulness?"

He answered: It is not as Moses wrote and you have read. He said in his first book, "He put him to sleep,"* but only in his perception, for he said through his prophet, "I will make their hearts heavy that they may not pay attention and may not see."†

The luminous Epinoia hid herself in Adam, and the chief Archon wanted to draw her out of his rib. But the luminous Epinoia cannot be seized and though Darkness chased her, it failed to catch her. So he extracted a portion of his power from him. He made a second creature in the form of a woman and according to the likeness of Epinoia as she had appeared to him. He joined the portion which he had taken from the power of the man to the female creature, but not in the way Moses said — "his rib."

Adam saw the woman beside him. In that instant, the luminous Epinoia appeared and lifted the veil which lay over his mind. He became sober from the intoxication of Darkness. He recognized his counter-image and said: "This is truly bone from my bones and flesh from my flesh." Thus man will leave father and mother and will cleave to his wife. They will be one flesh.

Our sister Sophia descended in innocence to rectify her deficiency. Therefore she is called Life, the mother of the living. Through the Foreknowledge of the Sovereignty and through her, they have tasted perfect *gnosis*. I appeared in the form of an eagle on the Tree of Knowledge, which is the Epinoia of the Pure Light,

* *Genesis*, 2:21.

† *Isaiah*, 6:10.

so that I might teach them and awaken them from the depths of sleep. They were both in a fallen condition and they beheld their nakedness. Epinoia appeared to them as a light and awakened their thinking.

When Ialdabaoth saw that they shunned him, he cursed his earth. He discovered the woman as she was preparing herself for her husband. Even though he did not understand the mystery which had come to pass through the holy decree, he was lord over her, and they feared to blame him. He showed his angels his own ignorance and cast them out of paradise and clothed them in gloomy darkness. The chief Archon saw the virgin who stood next to Adam, and he saw that the luminous Epinoia of life had manifested in her. Yet Ialdabaoth was full of ignorance. But when the Pronoia of the All saw it, she sent and snatched Life out of Eve.

Then the chief Archon seduced her and begot two sons, Eloim and Yave, the first with the face of a bear and the second with a cat's countenance. The one is righteous, the other the opposite. Yave was set over fire and wind, and Eloim was placed over water and earth. But he called them Cain and Abel with the aim to deceive.

Until the present time sexual procreation has continued because of the chief Archon. He instilled sexual desire in her who belongs to Adam, for through intercourse he produced duplications of the bodies and inspired them with his contrary spirit.

He established two Archons over principalities so that they might rule over the tomb. When Adam recognized the image of his own foreknowledge, he begot the image of the Son of Man. He named him Seth after the manner of the race in the Aeons. Similarly, the mother also sent down her spirit — which is in her image and a duplicate of those abiding in the Pleroma — since she will prepare a dwelling-place for the Aeons who will descend. But the chief Archon made them drink of the water of forgetfulness so that they would not know whence they came. The seed tarried for a time assisting this process, so that when the Spirit descends from the Holy Aeons, he may raise him up and heal him of the deficiency. Then the whole Pleroma will become holy and without flaw.

I said to the Soter: "Lord, will all souls eventually be brought safely into the Pure Light?"

He answered: Profound thoughts have arisen in your mind and it is difficult to explain them to any save those who are from the Immovable Race. Those on whom the Spirit of Life descends and abides with power will be saved. They will become perfect and be worthy of glory. They will be purified of all wickedness and entanglement in evil. They will care only for incorruptibility and will be one-pointed in respect to it ever after, free from anger and envy, jealousy and desire and greed. They remain unaffected by anything except the bare condition of being incarnated, and that they bear while looking towards the time when they will be welcomed by the Receivers. They are worthy of the Imperishable Eternal Life and the Calling, for they bear and endure everything, that they may finish the good fight and inherit eternal life.

I said to him: "But, Lord, what of those upon whom the power and Spirit of Life descended yet who did not do these works? Will they be rejected?"

He answered: If the Spirit descended upon them, they will eventually be saved and will improve. The power descends on every human being, for without it no one can stand. When they are born, if the Spirit of Life increases and the power descends and strengthens the soul, it cannot be led astray by anyone through works of evil. But if the contrary Spirit descends, the soul is drawn by him and goes astray.

And I said: "Lord, where do these souls go when they depart from the flesh?"

He smiled and said to me: That soul in which the power rises superior to the despicable spirit is strong, and she flees from evil. She is rescued through the intervention of the Incorruptible One, and she is gathered up into the repose of the Aeons.

I asked: "Lord, where will the souls be of those who fail to know to whom they belong?"

He said: In those, the despicable spirit gained strength as they went astray. He weighs down the soul and draws her into evil works, and he plunges her into forgetfulness. When she comes forth from the body, she is given over to the authorities who came into being through the Archon. They bind her in chains, cast her into prison and consort with her until she is liberated from forgetfulness and gains *gnosis*. If she becomes perfect in this way, she is rescued.

And then I said: "Lord, how can the soul become smaller and return into the nature of its mother or into man?"

He rejoiced when I asked this, saying: Verily you are blessed, for you have understood! That soul is made to follow another one, for the Spirit of Life is in her. She is saved through him, and she does not incarnate again.

I asked: "Lord, there are those who knew but who have turned away. Whence go their souls?"

He answered: They are condemned to the place of the Angels of Poverty where there is no repentance. There they remain until the day when those who have blasphemed the Spirit are condemned to be punished eternally.

Then I asked: "Lord, whence came the despicable spirit?"

He said: The Mother-Father, overflowing with mercy, is the Holy Spirit in every way, the One who is merciful and who sympathizes with humanity. He is the Epinoia of the Pronoia of Light. He raised up the offspring of the perfect race. His thought is the eternal light of man. When the chief Archon recognized that human beings were exalted above him in the empyrean and that they reached beyond him in thinking, he desired to seize their thought, not knowing that he could not lay hold of thought which is beyond him.

He devised a plot with his authorities, which are his powers, and together they committed adultery with Sophia. Thus bitter fate was begotten through them, and it is the last of the terrible bonds. The bonds are such that they are dreadful to each other. It is adamant against her with whom the gods are united along with the angels and the demons and all generations until today. For that fate gave birth to every sin, injustice and blasphemy as well as the chain of forgetfulness and ignorance, every harsh command and serious sin, and overwhelming fear. Thus the whole creation was blinded so that none may know God who is above them. The chain of forgetfulness obscured their sins. They are bound with measure, time and moment, for fate is lord over everything.

But he repented for all that had come into being through him. So the chief Archon determined to bring a flood over the work of man. But the effulgence of the Light of Pronoia informed Noah, and he proclaimed it to all the sons of men. Those, however, who were strangers to him did not listen. It is not as Moses said, "They hid themselves in an ark,"* for not only Noah but also many other people from the Immovable Race hid themselves in a place. They hid themselves in a luminous cloud. He recognized his authority, and she who belongs to the Light was with him and shone on them because he had covered the whole earth with darkness.

The chief Archon made a plan with his powers. He dispatched his angels to the daughters of men so that they might take some of them for themselves and raise offspring for their enjoyment. At first they did not succeed. When they met with failure, they convened and devised a plan. They created a despicable spirit — resembling the descending Spirit — in order to pollute souls. These angels transformed their appearances into the likenesses of the husbands of the daughters of men and filled them with the conjured spirit of Darkness and with evil. They distributed gold and silver, copper and iron, as gifts along with other metals and all kinds of things. They steered the people who followed them into terrible troubles, leading them astray with innumerable deceptions. The people aged without enjoyment, and they died without knowing the God of Truth. So the whole creation became enslaved forever, from the foundation of the world until today. They took wives and begot children out of Darkness and in the likeness of their spirit. They closed their hearts and hardened themselves through the hardness of the despicable spirit even until now.

Thus I, the perfect Pronoia of the Pleroma, transform myself into my seed, for I existed in the beginning, taking every path. I am the refulgence of the Light. I am the remembrance of the Pleroma.

I entered the realm of Darkness and there persevered until I found the centre of the prison. And the foundations of chaos trembled, and I veiled myself to them because of their wickedness, and they failed to recognize me.

Then I returned a second time and I travelled about. I came out from those who are of the Light, which is even myself, the remembrance of the Pronoia. I entered the centre of Darkness and the interior of Hades, for I sought to perform my task. Again the foundations of chaos shook, as if to collapse upon those who are in chaos and to annihilate them. I retreated to my tap-root of

* *Genesis*, 7:7.

Light, lest they be destroyed before the time.

Again a third time I went — even I, the Light which exists in the Light, the remembrance of the Pronoia — that I might enter the heart of Darkness and the centre of Hades. I made my countenance replete with the light of the summation of their Aeon. And so I entered into the centre of their prison, which is the prison of the body. And I said: "He who hears, let him arise from deep sleep." Then the sleeper wept and shed tears. Wiping bitter tears from his eyes, he said: "Who calls my name, and whence comes this hope emanated even while I am in chains in this prison?" And I said: "I am the Pronoia of the Pure Light. I am the intellection of the Virginal Spirit, he who raised you up to the place of honour. Arise and remember! It is you who hearkened: follow your root, which is even I, the Merciful One. Guard yourself against the Angels of Poverty and the demons of chaos and against all those who ensnare you. Beware of the deep sleep and the walls which enclose Hades."

And I raised him up and sealed him in the Light of the water with five seals in order that Death might not have power over him from this time on.

And behold, now I shall ascend to the perfect Aeon. I have related everything to you within your hearing. I have uttered everything that you must write down and give secretly to your companion spirits, for this is the mystery of the Immovable Race.

And the Soter presented these things that he might record them and keep them secure. And he said: Cursed be everyone who will exchange these things for a gift or for food, for drink or for clothing, or for any other thing.

These things were presented to him in a mystery, and at once he disappeared from him. And John went to his fellow disciples and told them what the Soter had said to him.

Jesus Christ, Amen.

The Secret Teaching According to John

EVANGELIUM VERITATIS

The Gospel of Truth is Joy
For those who have received from the Father of Truth
The Gift of knowing him
Through the power of the Word
Which emerged from the *pleroma*
That exists in the Thought and the Mind of the Father.
This Word is called the Soter (Saviour)
Since it is the name of the work he must perform
For the redemption of those ignorant of the Father,
While the name of the Gospel is the Proclamation of Hope,
Being a discovery for those who seek for him.

For the All searched about for the One
From whom it came, and the All was within him,
The Incomprehensible and Inconceivable One,
Who transcends every thought.
Ignorance of the Father fostered anguish and terror,
And the anguish condensed into a fog
Until none could see into it.
Thus Error grew powerful,
Fashioning its matter in the Void.*

Since it did not know the Truth,
It undertook to make a creature,
Attempting to forge in Beauty a surrogate for Truth.
This was no humiliation for him,
The Incomprehensible and Inconceivable One,
For the anguish and oblivion and creaturely tissue of lies
Were nothing: Truth is immutable, immovable
And perfected in Beauty. Therefore, despise Error.
Without any root, it fell into a fog concerning the Father,

* The Coptic *petschueit* is equivalent to the Greek *kenoma*, void, nothingness.

Even while it was nurturing works of oblivion and terror
By which to ensnare those of the centre* and imprison them.
Oblivion, offspring of Error, was not revealed.
It is nothing from the Father and did not emerge under him,
Although it came into existence because of him.
What arose in him is *gnosis,*
Which revealed itself so that oblivion might vanish
So that the Aeons might know the Father.
Since oblivion arose because he was not known,
When he comes to be known,
Oblivion will perish from that moment onward.

This is the Gospel of Him Who Is Sought,
Which, revealed to those who are perfected
Through the mercy of the Father,
Is the Hidden Mystery, Jesus the Christos.
Through it, he enlightened those in darkness;
Out of oblivion, he illumined them, showing a way.
This way is the Truth he taught.

Thus Error was enraged with him and persecuted him,
Was distressed at him, and came to naught.
He was nailed to a tree:
He became the fruit of the Knowledge of the Father,
Which was not destructive to those who partook of it.
Indeed, those who ate were filled with joy at the discovery.
He found them in himself, and they found him in themselves,
The Incomprehensible and Inconceivable One,
The Father, the Perfect One, the One who
Formed the *pleroma* which is ever within him
And ever has need of him, since he retained its perfection
Within himself and did not pass it to the *pleroma.*
The Father is not jealous, for what jealousy
Could exist between himself and his members?

* "Those of the centre" probably refers to those Aeons who took on human form.

If the Aeon had received their perfection,
They could not come to the Father
Who retains their fulfilment within himself
As assurance of their return to him
Along with *gnosis* singular in perfection.
He formed the All, and the All is within him,
And the All needed him.

Just as someone whom many do not know
May wish them to know and love him,
What did the All have need of
If not of *gnosis* regarding the Father?
He became a tranquil and devoted guide;
He entered the schools and taught
As Master of the Word.
Wise men — wise in their own estimation —
Approached him and put him to the test.
But he unmasked them because they were foolish,
And they hated him for they were not truly wise.

After these, the little children also came,
Those to whom Knowledge of the Father belongs.
Given strength,* they learned to discern
The manifestations of the Father.
They knew, and they were known.
They glorified, and they were glorified.
In their hearts there was revealed
The Living Book of the Living,
The one inscribed in the Thought and the Mind
Of the Father, which was in the incomprehensible parts
Of the Father from before the foundation of the All,
That book which no one can take, for it is saved
For him who would be slain to take it.
None could have appeared to believe in redemption

* The Coptic *tok* (strengthen, consolidate) is used metaphorically to mean 'baptize.'

Until the intervention of that book.
Thus the Merciful One, the Faithful One, Jesus,
Patiently bore sufferings until he had taken that book,
Knowing that his death is life for many.

Just as the fortune of a deceased master of a house
Lies secreted in his unread will,
So with the All which remained hidden
While the Father of the All was invisible,
He who is self-existent, from whom all spaces* come.
For this reason Jesus appeared,
Took up the book and was nailed to a tree.
He promulgated the Father's decree on the cross.
How great the Teaching!
He drew himself down to death
And was clothed in eternal life.
Having stripped off the rags of perishability,
He put on imperishability which none can take away.
Entering the empty spaces of the Terror,
He passed into those stripped naked by Oblivion,
Since he is Knowledge and perfection,
And proclaimed what abides in the heart of the Father,
To teach those who will receive the Teaching.

Those who will receive the Teaching are the Living
Who are inscribed in the Book of the Living,
And they receive the Teaching about themselves.
They receive it from the Father and turn again to him.
Since the perfection of the All is in the Father,
The All needs must ascend to him.
If one gains Knowledge, he receives what are his own
And gathers them to himself.

---

* The Coptic *maeit* (way) has the meaning of 'space' and corresponds to the concept of Aeon.

But he who is ignorant is in need and his lack is enormous,
For he is devoid of that which will make him perfect.
The perfection of the All is in the Father,
And so the All must ascend to him,
And each one must repossess his own.
He has named them in advance, preparing them
To give to those who came forth from him.

Those whose names were known by him in advance
Have been called at the end;
One who has Knowledge
Is one whose name has been uttered by the Father.
One whose name remains unuttered is ignorant,
For how could one hear his name if it has not been called?
He who is ignorant until the end
Is a creature of Oblivion,
Doomed to vanish along with it.
Otherwise, how can it be that these wretches
Have no name and hear no call?
The man of *gnosis* is from above.
If he is called, he hears,
And he turns to him who calls
And ascends to him,
Knowing the nature of the call.
Having this knowledge, he performs the will
Of the one who called him,
And, wishing to be pleasing to him,
He gains repose.

Each one's name comes to him.
He who has Knowledge knows whence he came
And whither he is going,
Like a man who, having become drunk,
Turns away from his drunkenness
And comes back to himself
And sets right what are his own.

He has rescued many from Error.
He has preceded them to the places they abandoned
When they succumbed to Error
Because of the vastitude of the one
Who encompasses all spaces
While there is naught that encircles him.
Wondrous it is that they were in the Father
And failed to know him
And that they came forth of themselves,
Being unable to understand or even to know
The One in whom they were.
Yet his will thus emerged from him,
For he revealed it for Knowledge
In which all its emanations agree.

This is the Knowledge of the Living Book
Which he revealed to the Aeons to the endmost letter,
Revealing that they are neither vowels nor consonants,
So that none can read them and think of foolish things.
They are letters of Truth
Pronounced by them alone who know them.
Each letter is a perfect Thought
Like a perfect book,
Since they are letters written by the Unity,
The Father having inscribed them for the Aeons
So that by reading them, they might know the Father.

His Wisdom contemplates the Word;
His Teaching expresses it;
His Knowledge has revealed it;
His Forbearance crowns it;
His Joy harmonizes with it;
His Glory exalts it;
His Image has unveiled it;
His Repose gathers it into itself;
His Love has made a vesture for it;

His Fidelity has embraced it.
Thus the Word of the Father pervades the All
As the fruit of his Heart
And the impression of his Will.
It upholds the All;
It chooses the All,
And takes on the form of the All,
Purifying it and gathering it back
Into the Father, into the Mother,
Jesus, infinitude of gentleness.

The Father uncovered his breast
— His breast is the Holy Spirit —
And revealed what is hidden in him
— What is hidden is his Son —
So that through the compassion of the Father
The Aeons may know him, cease searching
And come to abide there in him,
Knowing that this is the Repose.
When he had filled that deficiency,
He annihilated form,
And this form is the world which enslaved him.
Deficiency is found wherever there is envy and dissension.
But the abode of Unity is Plenitude.
Deficiency came into being
Where the Father was unknown;
When, therefore, the Father is known,
Deficiency ceases from that moment forever.
Just so with the ignorance of a person:
When he awakens to Knowledge, ignorance dissolves.
As darkness vanishes with the appearance of light,
Deficiency vanishes in Plenitude.
From that moment on form is no longer apparent,
For it vanishes in the union with Unity,
And its works are scattered about.
In time Unity will perfect the spaces,

And in Unity each one will attain himself.
Through knowledge, he will purify himself
From multiplicity into Unity,
Burning up matter within himself like a flame,
Like darkness consumed by Light,
Like death consumed by Life.

If in truth these things have happened to each of us,
We must see that the house will be
Holy and silent for the Unity.
As when some people move out of a neighbourhood
Leaving jars that are not sound:
They would destroy them
And the master of the place would suffer no loss.
Rather, he would rejoice,
For the bad jars are replaced
By jars perfect and full.
Such is the judgement which has come from above,
Passing judgement on each one
Like a double-edged sword cutting on either side.
When the Word descended into the midst,
The Word which is in hearts of those who utter it,
It was no empty sound but an embodiment.

Great Confusion reigned among the jars
Because some were left empty, others full,
Some were tended, others poured out,
Some were sanctified and others shattered.
All the spaces were shaken and disturbed,
Having neither order nor stability.
Error was agitated, not knowing what to do.
Error was grieved as in mourning,
Torturing itself because it knew nothing.
When Knowledge drew close to it,
Error was annihilated with all its emanations,
For Error is void and has nothing inside.

Truth entered into the midst,
And all the emanations knew it,
Greeting the Father in Truth and the perfect power
That unites them with the Father.
All beings love the Truth
For Truth is the mouth of the Father,
And his tongue is the Holy Spirit.
He who is united with Truth is conjoined
To the mouth of the Father by his tongue
When he receives the Holy Spirit.
This is the manifestation of the Father
And his revelation to the Aeons:
He unveiled what was hidden in him,
And he explained it.
For who receives, if not the Father alone?
All spaces are his emanations.
They knew that they emerged from him
Like children from a grown man.
They knew that they had not received
A name or a form,
Each of which the Father sires;
But when they gain form through his Knowledge,
Even though they are in him,
They still know him not.
The Father, however, is perfect
And knows all the spaces within him.
Whenever he wills,
He manifests whomsoever he will,
Giving him name and form.
Thus, those who are before they are manifested
Are ignorant of him who gestated them.

I do not mean that they are nothing
Who have yet to come into being;
Rather they repose in him
Who wills their existence

Whenever he will it,
Like the time that is to come.
Before all things appear,
He knows what he will bring forth,
But hitherto unmanifested fruit
Knows nothing and does nothing.
Thus, every space which is in the Father
Is from the One Who Is
And who established it out of what is not.
He who is rootless is fruitless.
He thinks to himself, "I have come to be,"
And yet he will perish by himself.
Thus, he who never was shall never be.
What then did he intend to think?
This: "I am like shadows and phantoms of the night."
When the Light shines upon the Terror
Which chained that being,
He knows that it is nothing.

They were ignorant of the Father,
For he was the One they did not see.
It was Terror
— Disturbance, instability, doubt and division —
And illusions at work because of it,
Along with empty fictions
That plunged them in sleep and distressing dreams.
Either they are fleeing some place
Or they are exhausted,
Having chased after others,
Or they are embroiled in brawls,
Throwing punches and receiving blows,
Or they have plummeted from the heights
And tried to soar wingless.
Sometimes, it is as if they were being murdered,
Though no one is really pursuing them,
Or they are killing their neighbours,

Having been stained with their blood.

Those who experience all these things
Awaken, and they see nothing.
Though in the midst of disturbances,
They are nothing.
This is the way of those
Who cast ignorance aside like sleep,
Esteeming it as nothing,
Not giving substance to its works,
Abandoning it like a dream in the night,
For Knowledge of the Father is like the dawn.
Thus each one has acted,
As though asleep at the time,
When immersed in ignorance.
And thus each one has come to Knowledge
As if rising to wakefulness.
Happy is he who comes to himself;
Blessed is he who opens the eyes of the blind,
For the Spirit pursued him in haste
And awakened him.
Giving a hand to one prone on the ground,
He stood him up on his feet,
For he had not yet arisen.
He gave them Knowledge,
Knowledge of the Father,
And revelation of the Son.

When they had seen and heard him,
He allowed them to savour him,
And to smell and touch the Beloved Son.
When he had appeared,
Teaching them about the Father,
The Incomprehensible One,
And breathing into them
What is in the mind when doing his will,

108

Many received the Light
And turned to him.
Men of *hyle** were strangers
And did not see his likeness,
Not having known him.
For he appeared in fleshly garments,
Although nothing barred his path,
Which was incorruptible and irresistible.
Though speaking new things,
He spoke what abides in
The Heart of the Father
And uttered the flawless Word.
Light discoursed through his mouth
And his voice gave birth to Life.
He bestowed upon them thought and wisdom,
Mercy, salvation and the powerful spirit
From the infinitude and gentleness of the Father.
He ended punishment and torture,
For these turned many from his face,
In Error and bondage, needing mercy.
He destroyed them with power
And confounded them with Knowledge.
He became the Way for those lost,
Gnosis for those ignorant,
A goal for those searching,
A pillar for those wavering,
And purity for those defiled.

He is the shepherd who left
The ninety-nine sheep which had not strayed.
He went searching for the one lost sheep,
And rejoiced when he found it,
For ninety-nine is a number

* *Hyle*, Greek for 'matter,' is contrasted with *pneuma,* 'spirit.' Hylic souls are those attracted unnaturally towards darkness and ignorance, and pneumatic souls are drawn to the light of *gnosis.*

Of the left hand which holds it.
When the one is found,
The whole number passes to the right hand.
So with him who lacks the One:
The right takes what was deficient
From the left, and with the One
The number becomes one hundred.*
This is the sign of the One
Who is in their sound — the Father.
Even on the Sabbath, he laboured
For the sheep fallen into the pit.
He gave life to the sheep,
Bringing it out of the pit
So that you might know inwardly
— You sons of interior Knowledge —
The meaning of the Sabbath,
When salvation should never be idle,
And so that you may speak
From the day that is above
Which knows no night
And from the Light which never fails
Because it is perfect.
Say, then, from your hearts
That you are the perfect day,
For in you dwells
The Light that does not fail.
Speak of Truth to those who seek it,
And of Knowledge to those who sin in Error.
Support the slumber,
Reach out to those who are ill.
Feed those who hunger, comfort the weary;
Raise those who want to stand,
And awaken those who sleep.

---

* An ancient method of counting uses the left hand for tens and the right for hundreds.

You are the sword of understanding,
And if strength grows mightier through use,
Be concerned with yourselves.
Do not concern yourselves with other things
Already rejected by you.
Do not return to consume
What you have spewed forth.
Do not be moths or worms,
For you have already renounced all that.
Do not become a home for the devil,
For you have already destroyed him.
Lend not strength to obstacles
Which are already falling away.
Treat ill the unjust rather than the just,
For the unjust works in an unjust person,
But the righteous person
Performs his works among others.
So you also do the will of the Father,
Since you are from him.

The Father is gentle,
And whatsoever is in his will is good.
He recognized what is yours
That you might find rest in them.
For from the fruits
One knows the things that are yours,
Because the children of the Father
Are his aroma,
Being from the grace of his countenance.
The Father loves his aroma
And manifests it in every place,
And if it should mix with matter,
He gives his aroma to the Light
And while remaining in repose,
Makes it transcend every form and every sound.
For ears do not sense the aroma,

But the breath that contains the sense of smell
And draws the aroma to itself
Is submerged in the fragrance of the Father.
First it is sheltered,
Then taken to the place of its origin,
Where the first aroma has grown cold.
It is a kind of psychic form*
Which is like cold water spilled
Upon loose earth.
Those who look upon it think it is earth,
But then it dissolves again.
If drawn by a breath, it grows hot.
The aromas are cold from being divided;
For this reason faith came,
Doing away with division,
Bringing the warm *pleroma* of Love
So that the cold should never reign again
And there should be the unity of perfect thought.

This is the Word of the gospel
Of the discovery of the *pleroma,*
For those who await salvation
Descending from on high.
When the hope they wait for is waiting,
And they are shadowless Light,
Then the *pleroma* will be ready to come.
The weakness of matter
Did not spring from the limitlessness of the Father
Who is about to herald the time of deficiency,
Though none can say of the Incorruptible One
That he will come in this way.

* Most Gnostics recognized three broad aspects in the human constitution: *pneuma,* spirit (breath), *hyle,* matter, and *psyche,* soul (mind). The mind tends towards spirit or matter, thereby freeing or obscuring the imprisoned Light, eventually leading to total freedom or annihilation (irreversible imprisonment).

The depth of the Father was differentiated
And the thought of Error did not exist with him.
It is a thing that feebly falls
And can easily stand up again
In the discovery of him
Who has come to him whom he shall bring back.
The bringing back is named repentance.

For this reason incorruptibility breathed forth
To pursue the sinner so that he might rest.
Forgiveness is what remains for Light in imperfection,
The Word of the *pleroma.*
The physician hurries to the sick-bed,
For such is the will in him.
One who is imperfect does not hide it,
For the physician has what the sick man lacks.
Thus with the *pleroma* free of defect:
It fills up his lack,
Being provided to fill up what is lacking,
So that he can receive the grace.
When he was deficient, he lacked the grace,
And this is why there was diminution
In the place where grace is absent.
When what was diminished was received,
He revealed the imperfection as *pleroma,*
And this is the discovery of the Light of Truth
Which shone upon him, being immutable.

This is why Christ was talked about in their midst,
So that those disturbed might gain a bringing back,
And he might anoint them with ointment.
This ointment is the mercy of the Father,
Who will have mercy on them.
Those whom he has anointed
Are those who have become perfect.
Only full jars are usually anointed.

If the anointment of a jar is dissolved,
The jar is emptied, for it was imperfect
And the ointment leaked out.
Then a breath draws it,
By the power which is in itself.
But no seal is removed
From one without deficiency,
Nor is anything emptied therefrom.
If there is a lack,
The Father fills it again.
He is good, and he knows his seeds,
For he planted them in his paradise.
His paradise is his place of repose.

This is the perfect thought of the Father,
And these are the words of his meditation.
Every one of his words is the working
Of his will in the revelation of his Word.
When they were still in the abyss of his thought,
The Word which first came forth
Revealed them with a Mind that utters
The one Word in silence and grace.
It was called Thought,
For they were in it before being manifested.
It came forth first
At the time pleasing to the will of him who willed.
The will is the restful abode of the Father
Who is pleased with it.
Nothing occurs without him,
Nor without the will of the Father,
And yet his will is incomprehensible.
His impress is will,
And yet no one knows it,
Nor can one scrutinize it
In hopes of understanding it.
When he wills, what he wills is there

Even if they do not like its appearance.
But he knows the alpha and omega of all of them.
At their end he will question them face to face.
The end is gaining Knowledge about the Hidden One,
And this is the Father
From whom the beginning came forth,
And to whom all will return who have come from him.
They have come forth for the glory
And the joy of his Name.

Now the Name of the Father is the Son.
He first gave the Name to the one
Who came forth from him,
And he begot him as a son.
He gave him the Name which belonged to him.
He is the Father to whom everything belongs:
His is the Name; his is the Son.
It is possible for him to be seen,
But the Name is invisible,
For it alone is the Mystery
Of the Invisible
Which descends on ears filled with it.
Thus, in truth the Father's Name is unuttered,
Though it appears in the Son.

The Name is great.
Who can utter a Name for him
— The Great Name —
Save him alone to whom the name belongs,
Along with the Sons of the Name
In whom abides the Name of the Father
And who abide in his Name?
The Father is parentless,
And he alone begot a Name for himself
Even before the Aeons were brought forth
So that his name might preside over them as Lord,

The Name in Truth,
In his command through perfect power.
The Name is not just a word,
Nor is it an appellation,
For it is invisible.

He named himself because he sees himself,
And he alone had the power
To give himself a Name.
He who does not exist remains nameless,
For what name could be given?
Whosoever exists is also named,
And he knows himself.
But to name himself is reserved to the Father.
The Son is his Name.
He did not hide the Name away in his works,
For the Son existed,
And he alone was given the Name.
The Name is that of the Father,
And the Name of the Father is the Son.
Where else would mercy find a name?

But someone will say to his neighbour,
Who is it who can name
Himself before he existed,
As if a child did not receive
His name from his parents?
So we should reflect:
What is the Name?
It is the Name in Truth.
It is not a name given by a father,
For it is the real Name.
He did not gain this Name on loan,
As others do,
According to the form into which one is born.
But it is the real Name,

And no one gave it to him.
Nonetheless, he is Unnameable, Indescribable,
Until the one made perfect spoke of himself.
And this is he who has the power
To speak his Name and to see it.

When it pleased him that his Name
Should be his Son,
And he bestowed the Name on him
Who emerged from the depth,
He discoursed on secret things,
Knowing the Father to be free of taint.
For that reason he was brought forth
To speak about that home and place of repose
From which he had come forth,
And to glorify the *pleroma,*
The greatness of the Name
And the gentleness of the Father.
He will tell the place
From which each one sprang,
And he will speak of the realm
Of his essential being.
He will hasten to return again,
To come from the place where he stood,
Receiving a taste from these,
Gaining nutriment and growth.
And his own resting-place
Is his *pleroma.*

So all the Father's emanations are *pleromata,*
And their root is in the One
Who caused them to grow in himself.
He appointed their destinies.
Each one is manifested
So that through their own thought
They may be perfected.

For they send their thought to the place
Which is their root,
Which gathers them up to the heights of the Father.
They gain his head which is their repose,
And cleave to him
As if they joined his countenance through kisses.
But they do not manifest in this way,
For they did not step beyond themselves
Nor lack the glory of the Father
Nor think of him as little
Or harsh or filled with wrath,
But as a being free of evil,
Beyond disturbance, gentle,
Knowing all spaces even before
They came into existence,
And needing no instruction.

This is the way of those
Who hold something from on high
Of the Inconceivable Greatness.
They reach out towards
The One who is Alone, the Perfect One,
The One who is there for them.
They pass not into Hades,
Nor are they envious
Or filled with groaning,
Nor do they hold death within themselves,
For they rest in him who is at rest,
Neither striving
Nor struggling in the search for Truth.
They themselves are the Truth,
And the Father is within them
And they are in the Father,
Being perfect and undivided
In the absolutely Good One,
Deficient in nothing, always at rest,

Refreshed in the Spirit.
They heed their root.
They are concerned in that
Which unveils the root,
And suffer no loss to soul.
This is the place of the blessed:
This is their place.

For all others, then,
May they know in their places
That I cannot speak of other things,
Having come to abide in the place of rest.
There I shall come to concern myself
At every moment with the Father
Of all true brothers —
Those on whom the Father
Pours out his Love
And among whom
There is no lack of him.
They manifest in Truth,
For they live in true and eternal Life,
Speaking of the Perfect Light,
Filled with the seed of the Father,
Dwelling in his Heart
And in the *pleroma,*
While the Spirit rejoices in it
And glorifies the One
In whom it exists, for he is Good.
His children are perfect
And worthy of his Name,
For he is the Father.

Since they are children like this,
The Father loves them.

SONG OF THE PEARL

I

When I was but a little child,
Still living in my Father's dwelling — my Kingdom —
Relishing my teachers' splendour and riches,
My parents sent me away from the Orient
And my abode. Replete with equipment,
Drawn from the wealth of our treasury,
They packed me supplies, bulky yet light
Enough for me to bear alone:
With gold from the Abode of the Supreme Ones
And silver from Ganzak the Great;
With chalcedony taken from India
And agates from the Kingdom of Kushan.
And they girdled me with diamonds
Able to bite into iron.
They made me remove my refulgent robe,
Which they had woven for me out of their love,
Together with the purple toga
Woven and measured to fit my form.
And they sealed a pact with me, and inscribed it
In my heart, never to be forgotten:
"If thou shouldest descend to the Land of Egypt
And retrieve the pearl in the midst of the sea,
Surrounded now by the hissing serpent,
Then thou mayst don thy refulgent robe
And lay thy toga over it again,
And with thy Brother, who is our Second,
Become Crown Prince in our Kingdom."

II

Therewith I took leave of the Orient
And went down, with two guards' guidance,
For the way was dangerous and deceptive,
And I was too young to tread it alone.
I crossed the Land of Maishan,
Where merchants from the East meet,
And I came to the country of Babel
And stepped within the walls of Sarbug.
Into Egypt Land I descended
And my companions took leave of me.
Without wavering, I came to the dragon
And made my abode fast by his dwelling
Until he should slumber and fall asleep,
And I could seize the pearl from him.

And when I found myself utterly alone
And a stranger to those with whom I lived,
I suddenly espied a man of my clan,
A handsome noble from the Orient,
Youthful, a Son of the Anointed,
And he came and made friends with me.
I made him my friend and companion,
And let him join in my endeavour.
He warned me against the Egyptians
And against consorting with the Unclean.
Nonetheless, I clothed myself in their manner,
Lest they came to have a suspicion
That I had come from another world
In order to seize the pearl
And arouse the serpent against me.

Despite precaution, somehow or other,
They saw I was not one of them.
They approached me with cunning
And offered me their food to eat,

And I forgot I was the Son of a King
And made obeisance unto their king.
I completely forgot the pearl for which
My parents had first sent me.
Because their food was heavy,
I sank into deep sleep's oblivion.

III

But everything which happened to me
Reached my parents' ears: they grieved.
A proclamation went forth throughout our Kingdom
Summoning everyone to come to our gate:
All the Kings and Lords of Parthia
And all the nobles of the Orient.
They made a resolution for my sake
Never to abandon me in Egypt.

And they composed a letter to me
In which each noble inscribed his name:
"From thy Father, the King of Kings,
And thy Mother, Mistress of the Orient,
And from thy Brother, our Second in station,
To thee, our Son in Egypt, greetings.
Arise! Wake from thy slumber; hearken
And listen to the words of our letter.
Remember thou art the Son of Kings.
Look upon this slavery and upon whom you serve!
Remember the pearl, the gem for which
Thou wert dispatched to Egypt.
Remember also thy refulgent robe;
Remember thy glorious toga
With which thou shalt adorn thyself
That thy name be written in the Book of Heroes.
Then with our deputy, thy Brother,
Thou shalt share this kingdom, thy heritage."

IV

The King took up the letter,
Sealing it with his right hand,
Safeguarding it from the wicked of Babel
And from the savage demons of Sarbug.
It soared in the form of an eagle,
King of birds. It flew and alighted
Beside me and was transformed into speech.
I awoke at the sound of its flight;
At its voice I arose from slumber.
I embraced it and kissed it, and loosed
Its seal to read: the words of the letter
Matched those inscribed in my heart.

I remembered I was the Son of Kings
And that my freedom demanded
Translation into reality.
I remembered the pearl for which
I had been sent to the Land of Egypt.
So I began to weave my spell
Upon the noisome, fierce, snorting dragon.
I lulled him into somnambulance, into sleep,
By naming my Father's Name over him,
And the Name of our Second in Rank
And the Name of my Mother, Queen of the Orient.
I seized the pearl and turned around
To return to the abode of my Father.
I tore away their dirty, shabby garments
And dropped them there in Egypt Land.

I made my way towards the Light
Of our homeland, always to the East.
My letter, my own self-awakener,
Lay before me on the selfsame road.
Just as it had aroused me with its voice,
Now it guided me with its light.

Like ochre characters on Chinese silk,
Its shining form streamed out ahead,
And its voice of encouragement gave
Direction, drawing me on with love.
Steadily forward, I passed through Sarbug
And through Babel, which lay on my left,
And I came in time to Maishan the Great,
The abode of the diverse merchant traders,
By the shores of the sea.
The refulgent robe I had laid aside
And the toga which was wrapped round it,
From the lofty peaks of Hyrcania,
My parents had sent hither to me
Through the offices of their chancellery,
Wholly trusted for their loyalty.

V

Although I had forgotten its majesty,
Since I left my Father when only a child,
Suddenly as I beheld it before me,
It became a reflection of myself.
I beheld its refulgence within myself,
And beheld myself in it, facing me,
For though we were twain in diversity,
We were one in similarity.
And I saw the Chancellors,
Who brought the robe, in similar way:
They were two, yet equal in their form.
The seal of the King was impressed on them,
For through them he had restored to me
My treasure along with all my riches,
My refulgent robe with its embroidery,
A splendour born of glorious colours,
A marvel of gold, graced with beryls,
And chalcedony crested with agates
And variegated sardonyxes.

The robe, prepared in sublimity,
Its needlework everywhere strengthened
With stones of adamant, and the image
Of the King of Kings, life-size, painted
Across its length. And all its colours
Reflected like stones of sapphire.

VI

I saw that in all its parts
The motion of my *Gnosis* started up,
And commenced to prepare
As if it were about to speak.
I heard the music of its melodies
Whispered as it descended to me:
"I belong to the swiftest servants
Who were raised before my Father.
I have felt my stature grow within
In accordance with his labours."
Its gestures were royal, reaching out
In my direction, hastening
From its deliverers' hands
For me to receive it. I too felt urged
By my love to return its welcome.
I stretched myself forth and received it.
I covered myself in its splendour
Of colours, wrapping myself all around
In my toga of brilliant hues.

I clothed myself and made ascension
To the Gates of Greeting and of Homage.
With head bowed, I made obeisance
To the Father's Glory, who sent me
And whose commands I had fulfilled.
He also had fulfilled his promise,

And at the gate of his satraps
I was made companion of his nobles,
For he rejoiced and received me,
And I was with him in his Kingdom.
Accompanied by the sound of celestes,
His servants praised him for his promise
That at the Gate of the King of Kings
With the offering of the pearl of mine,
I would with my Brother appear before the King.

Acta Thomae, 108-113

THE VOICE DIVINE

The Voice of the Soul

Is man a god? What strange deceit is here!
Behold this prodigy divine appear
Vested in weakness, with disgrace his crown —
What foe has stripp'd him of his old renown?
Not king but captive now, to sense a thrall,
And, exiled far from his imperial hall,
The sacred accents of the heavenly shore,
The harp's harmonious strains, he hears no more.

The Voice Divine

O'er all that lives his once established right
Peace to its empire gave beneath my sight;
Ye slaves who now your ancient lord subdue,
Peace when he seeks must be implored of you!
Once from life's stream he drew, which heard my voice,
And, leaping down, did earth with fruits rejoice;
What waters now will make that desert bear?
Tears from his eyes alone, descending there!

Man is the secret sense of all which seems;
That other doctrines are but idle dreams,
Let Nature, far from all contention, own,
While his grand doom is by her day-star shown.
To vaster laws adjusted, he shall reign,
Earth for his throne, and his star-crown attain,
The Universal world his empire wait,
A royal court restore his ancient state.

LOUIS CLAUDE DE SAINT-MARTIN

OM

GLOSSARY

Adam Kadmon	The divine prototype of cosmos and man
Aeon	A vast space or period of time; for Gnostics, an intelligence presiding over and manifesting in a space and time
Agape	Love, especially in the sense of friendliness or fraternal love; fellowship
Agnoia	Ignorance
Ain-Soph	Without limit; the Absolute and Unknowable Deity
Aionia Zoe	Eternal life
Aletheia	Truth
Anastasis	Resurrection
Anoia	*Annoia* or nescience
Archon	Ruler, chief; a lesser intelligence
Autogenes, Autogenetos	Self-born
Brahma Vach	Divine Speech; the Word; highest wisdom
Charis	Grace
Chréstos	One who aspires to Spiritual Truth
Christos	Literally, the anointed; one filled with the Spirit of Truth
Dekas	Literally, the Tenth; a plane of existence and an Aeon
Eirene	Peace
Enneas	Ninth; a plane of existence and an Aeon
Ennoia	Thought; ideation; concept
Gnosis	Knowledge; spiritual insight
Helidomas	Seventh; a plane of being and an Aeon
Homopneumata	Like spirits, fellow spirits; of the same breath
Hyle	Matter; corporeality

Kabbalah	Literally, tradition; knowledge of the inner mystical meaning of the Torah and of Jewish religious practices; also Qabbalah, Cabala
Logion, Logia	Saying; utterance
Logos	Literally, word; cause; reason
Mantram	Incantation; sacred invocation
Monogenes	Only-begotten
Mysteria	Mysteries; secret teachings of Jesus; the subjects of those teachings
Nous	Mind, intelligence
Pentas	The Fifth; a plane of being and an Aeon
Phronesis	Practical wisdom, prudence
Pleroma	Fullness; the pure potentiality of manifest existence; the Divine Light
Pneuma	Breath, spirit
Prognosis	Foreknowledge
Pronoia	Forethought, providence, conception
Psyche	Soul, self-consciousness
Sephirothal Tree	The ten Sephiroth of the Kabbalah depicted in the form of a tree
Shekinah	The Divine Voice; the creative power of the Divine
Sophia	Wisdom
Soter	Saviour, used of the Christos
Sufi	A Muslim mystic
Synesis	Insight, understanding
Syzygies	Pairs of creative intelligences
Tikkun	Literally, restoration; the basic feature of redemption according to Isaac Luria
Zoe	Life

THE PYTHAGOREAN SANGHA

THE JEWEL IN THE LOTUS edited by Raghavan Iyer

THE GRIHASTHA ASHRAMA by B. P. Wadia

THE MORAL AND POLITICAL THOUGHT
    OF MAHATMA GANDHI by Raghavan Iyer

THE BHAGAVAD GITA edited by Raghavan Iyer

THE MAITREYA ACADEMY

PARAPOLITICS — TOWARD THE CITY OF MAN by Raghavan Iyer

THE PLATONIC QUEST by E. J. Urwick

OBJECTIVITY AND CONSCIOUSNESS by Robert Rein'l

SANGAM TEXTS

THE BEACON LIGHT by H. P. Blavatsky

THE SERVICE OF HUMANITY by D. K. Mavalankar

HIT THE MARK by W. Q. Judge

THE PROGRESS OF HUMANITY by A. P. Sinnett

CONSCIOUSNESS AND IMMORTALITY by T. Subba Row

THE GATES OF GOLD by M. Collins

THE LANGUAGE OF THE SOUL by R. Crosbie

THE ASCENDING CYCLE by G. W. Russell

THE DOCTRINE OF THE BHAGAVAD GITA by Bhavani Shankar

THE LAW OF SACRIFICE by B. P. Wadia

SACRED TEXTS

RETURN TO SHIVA (from the *Yoga Vasishtha Maharamayana*)

THE GATHAS OF ZARATHUSTRA — The Sermons of Zoroaster

TAO TE CHING by Lao Tzu

SELF-PURIFICATION (Jaina Sutra)

THE DIAMOND SUTRA (from the Final Teachings of the Buddha)

THE GOLDEN VERSES OF PYTHAGORAS
(with the commentary of Hierocles)

IN THE BEGINNING — The Mystical Meaning of Genesis

THE GOSPEL ACCORDING TO THOMAS
(with complementary texts)

THE SEALS OF WISDOM — The Essence of Islamic Mysticism
by Ibn al-ʿArabi

CHANTS FOR CONTEMPLATION by Guru Nanak

INSTITUTE OF WORLD CULTURE

THE SOCIETY OF THE FUTURE by Raghavan Iyer

THE RELIGION OF SOLIDARITY by Edward Bellamy

THE BANQUET (Percy Bysshe Shelley's translation
of Plato's *Symposium*)

THE DREAM OF RAVAN *A Mystery*

THE LAW OF VIOLENCE AND THE LAW OF LOVE by Leo Tolstoy

THE RECOVERY OF INNOCENCE by Pico Iyer

UTILITARIANISM AND ALL THAT by Raghavan Iyer

NOVUS ORDO SECLORUM by Raghavan Iyer

The CGP emblem identifies this book as a production of Concord Grove Press, publishers since 1975 of books and pamphlets of enduring value in a format based upon the Golden Ratio. This volume was typeset in Journal Roman Bold and Bodoni Bold, printed on acid-free paper and Smyth sewn. A list of publications can be obtained from Concord Grove Press, P. O. Box 959, Santa Barbara, California 93102 U.S.A.